Rocky Mountain

GARDEN SURVIVAL GUIDE

Susan J. Tweit

Susan J. Tweit

D0367560

FULCRUM PUBLISHING

Golden, Colorado

For my mom,
who taught me the love of flowers,
wild and domestic.
And for Bev,
who tends the prettiest garden in our town.

Text copyright © 2004 Susan Tweit

Library of Congress Cataloging-in-Publication Data

Tweit, Susan J.
The Rocky Mountain garden survival guide / Susan J. Tweit.
     p. cm.
Includes index.
ISBN 1-55591-507-8
 1. Gardening—Rocky Mountains Region. I. Title.
SB453.2.R63T84 2004
635.9'0978--dc22
     2003024556

ISBN 1-55591-507-8
Printed in
0 9 8 7 6 5 4 3 2 1

Editorial: Cathy Wilkinson Barash, Faith Marcovecchio, Katie Raymond
Design: Ann W. Douden, Anne Clark
Cover illustration: Mindy Dwyer

FULCRUM PUBLISHING
16100 Table Mountain Parkway, Suite 300
Golden, Colorado 80403
(800) 992-2908 • (303) 277-1623
www.fulcrum-books.com

Contents

CONTENTS

V

1

Introduction

You can identify Rocky Mountain gardeners by the stories they tell: the wet spring snow that caused prized trees and shrubs to collapse, the grasshoppers that mowed down the emerging vegetable sprouts, the July hail that flattened every flower in the garden, the deer that munched the columbines, and the winter winds that toppled the spruce in the front yard. Gardening in this scenic but difficult region is all about weather. Like a good cutting horse or a high-tech mountain bike, Rocky Mountain weather can turn on a dime, from drought to deluge, searing heat to subfreezing cold, dead calm to roaring Chinooks. Weather is not a Rocky Mountain gardener's only challenge, however. The region's spectacular scenery makes for topographic trials and soils that are, by and large, undeveloped. The region's arid climate means that watered and fertilized gardens are a magnet for pests of every size from microbes to moose. Add an increasing number of invasive weeds, the reality of water shortages, and the threat of global climate change, and painting the yard green begins to seem very attractive.

If you're wondering how to nurture a thriving garden in the adverse conditions of the Rocky Mountain region, this book is for you. It's a compendium of one-page tips for dealing with regional gardening challenges, interspersed with brief essays explaining the fundamentals of garden ecology, design, and maintenance. It also includes suggested plants to deal with specific garden problems, plus public gardens and nurseries to visit for information and inspiration.

> *The balance of nature is ...*
> *a complex, precise,*
> *and highly integrated system of relationships*
> *between living things which cannot be safely*
> *ignored any more than the law of gravity*
> *can be defied with impunity by a man*
> *perched on the edge of a cliff.*
>
> —Rachel Carson, *Silent Spring*

The philosophy behind this book is simple: understanding the environment in which you're gardening allows you to work with the landscape and its living community instead of fighting against it, making gardening a source of pleasure and joy, not frustration and anger. This approach to gardening is informed by the science of ecology, the study of our place in nature. Understanding the ecology of your garden—the physical environment where it is located and the myriad relationships among the organisms that live around it and in it—is key to cultivating a healthy and thriving garden, especially in the difficult conditions of the Rocky Mountain region. A garden can be a pleasure, a personal sanctuary that nurtures and sustains you, even as you nurture it. A garden can provide your closest and most constant contact to nature—other than the microbes that live on and inside you. A garden can bring you home, reconnecting you to the intricate community of life that animates this beautiful Earth.

This book is divided into three major sections: "Geography," "Wild Weather and Changing Climates," and "Invaders."

 "Geography" focuses on the big picture, the physical environment of your garden including place, soil, and microclimate.

 "Wild Weather and Changing Climates" covers weather and climate in all of their permutations, including drought, flood, aridity, climate change, severe weather, and wildfire.

 "Invaders" surveys unwanted garden guests including invasive weeds, diseases, pests, and grazers of all sizes.

At the end of the book, appendices list seed companies and nurseries specializing in plants that thrive in the region, gardens open to the public, and Web sites and other sources of regionally appropriate garden information.

*May this book help you grow
the garden you desire!*

GEOGRAPHY

KNOWING the PLACE

You have to get over the color green. ...
—Wallace Stegner, "Thoughts in a Dry Land,"
*Where the Bluebird Sings to
the Lemonade Springs:
Living and Writing in the West*

No matter what your style of gardening—whether your secret desire is for an English cottage garden in arid Santa Fe, to grow avocados in Helena, or to go wild with native plants in suburban Boise—the first step in achieving gardening success is to understand place. Find out where your garden fits in the larger geographic sense and discover the physical attributes of your specific location.

With elevations ranging from 3,439 feet above sea level at Calgary, Alberta, to Colorado's Mount Elbert at 14,433 feet, the gardening environment varies enormously across the region. Sometimes the change in topographic relief is so abrupt it is almost as if the Earth hiccupped, heaving mountains out of flat plains. From downtown Salt Lake City at 4,260 feet in elevation, for example, the Wasatch Front soars to 10,500-foot Mount Olympus, a mere eleven miles away. That's a change in environments akin to traveling from Albuquerque to northern Canada.

Still, commonalities unite this diverse region. Much of it is arid or semiarid, with average annual precipitation varying from less than seven inches to more than sixteen. Topography is often sloping or dangerously steep, and exposure is sometimes severe. Potential solar radiation is generally high as is average wind speed. Bone-chilling cold winters alternate with searing hot summers. Soils are generally thin and lacking in nutrients.

Knowing the region tells you what general gardening conditions to expect. Learning to read the details of place allows you to figure out what plants will thrive where.

What's in a Zone?

Understanding the USDA Plant Hardiness Zone map is as basic to gardening as knowing how to use a good shovel. Horticulturists developed this scheme for summarizing environmental information under the leadership of Henry T. Skinner, the second director of the United States National Arboretum, compiling data on lowest average winter temperatures and plant hardiness and then defining eleven Hardiness Zones for the contiguous United States and Canada.

Each zone covers a ten-degree difference in average annual minimum temperatures. In Zone 1, for instance, the climate characteristic of Fairbanks, Alaska, winter minimums average less than -50° F, while in Zone 11, on the opposite side of the continent in coastal Florida, winter minimum temperatures average above 40° F. Under the original system, the Rocky Mountain region fell into Zones 3 (average winter minimums of -40° to -30° F) through 5 (-20° to -10° F), with a few warmer exceptions at the low-elevation edges of the region. A plant labeled as hardy in Zones 3–9 will thrive throughout the region; one marked with Zones 7–9 likely won't.

In 1990, each of the original zones was split into two subzones of five-degree differences in average minimum temperature, thus Zone 5 became Zone 5a (-20° to -15° F) and Zone 5b (-15° to -10° F). Better data yielded a more precise zone map. For instance, the city of Denver jumped from Zone 5 to Zone 6a because of the urban heat island effect, where buildings and pavement store solar radiation, raising average temperatures.

What's Your Map Zone?

Using the USDA Hardiness Zone system is simple: locate your site on the USDA map (online at www.usna.usda.gov/Hardzone/ushzmap.html) and read the zone; then check the hardiness rating of the plants you are interested in.

The USDA Hardiness Zones indicate whether a particular plant can survive in your area's general climate. But other factors influence plant growth and survival as well. These factors include microclimate, soil type, precipitation, planting techniques, pH, fertilizer, plant-eaters of all sorts, diseases, and pollution. The zone system is one tool to understand place and plant adaptations; you'll need other tools, too.

▲ ▼ ▲ ▲ ▼ ▲ ▼ ▲ ▼ ▲ ▼ ▲ ▼ ▲ ▼

ROCKY MOUNTAIN REGION ZONES AND THEIR AVERAGE MINIMUM TEMPERATURE RANGES

    ZONE 3A: -40° to -35° F
    ZONE 3B: -35° to -30° F
    ZONE 4A: -30° to -25° F
    ZONE 4B: -25° to -20° F
    ZONE 5A: -20° to -15° F
    ZONE 5B: -15° to -10° F
    ZONE 6A: -10° to -5° F

▲ ▼ ▲ ▲ ▼ ▲ ▼ ▲ ▼ ▲ ▼ ▲ ▼ ▲ ▼

What's Your Actual Zone?

Interpreting the zone map for your specific location is only the beginning. Elevation, topography, and other factors influence the local climate and thus your zone.

Elevation comes into play because air is cooler at higher elevations: for every thousand feet of elevation gain, the average annual temperature drops about 4° F. Hence, there's a potential twenty-eight-degree drop in winter minimum temperatures, or three full zones between a garden at 7,000 feet in a valley and the summit of the 14,000-foot peaks just ten miles away. The Hardiness Zone map's scale cannot reflect such local variations.

Slope and exposure also affect zone. The farther north a site is from the equator, the more the sun's angle changes from summer—when the sun is more or less directly over-head at midday—to winter—when the midday sun is much closer to the southern horizon. Slopes that face north often receive no direct sunlight and remain snowbound all winter, while snow on south-facing slopes melts quickly, warmed by daily doses of solar radiation. Thus, the climate of adjacent north-facing and south-facing slopes may be several zones apart, as evidenced dramatically by their different plant communities, with forest or woodlands on the cooler slope and dry shrublands or grasslands on the warmer slope.

Solar exposure is critical to any site, no matter its slope. A high ridge, a building, or evergreen trees to the south cast shade all winter, chilling a Zone 6a site into a localized Zone 4a. That's like moving from Boise to Billings, a big change for any garden.

What's My Ecosystem?

Your native ecosystem tells you what environmental conditions affect your garden. (Ecosystem means the community of plants and animals that inhabit a place, plus its physical environment. The word comes from the Greek *ecos*, meaning "home," and *system*, reflecting the importance of the relationships between and among species and their environment. No matter where you live and what grows there now, the native ecosystem is the natural community that has adapted to your local environment.)

For instance, if your native ecosystem is short-grass prairie, the native plants give clues about the conditions. They are short, ground-hugging grasses and wildflowers adapted to low precipitation and long periods of drought, wet spring snowstorms, summer hail, windy and dry winters, hot summers, and clayey soils. (Trees grow naturally only in sheltered locations in these semiarid ecosystems.) This is the home system, the native conditions of your garden.

Or, suppose you live in a ponderosa pine ecosystem. The forest overstory tells you that the annual precipitation is ample enough to support native tree growth, while the sparse grass and shrub understory testifies to seasonal drought, periodic wildfires, and sandy, nutrient-poor soils. The same environmental challenges will shape your garden.

Tip   **Regional nature guidebooks such as the Sierra Club Naturalist's Guide Series or the Audubon Society Nature Guides explain native ecosystems. Nature centers, state and regional parks, and community colleges also offer classes on local ecosystems.**

▲ ▼ ▲ ▲ ▼ ▲ ▼ ▲ ▼ ▲ ▼ ▲ ▼ ▲ ▼

CULTURAL ECOSYSTEMS Established gardens and long-time gardeners are also a rich source of gardening wisdom. What are the heritage plants of your neighborhood, the plants that have flourished for many generations and give your area special character? What plants persist around abandoned house foundations or homesteads? These tough and characteristic plants are part of your cultural ecosystem.

▲ ▼ ▲ ▲ ▼ ▲ ▼ ▲ ▼ ▲ ▼ ▲ ▼ ▲ ▼

What's a Frost Pocket?
Reading the Landscape of Your Yard

A frost pocket is a low spot in the landscape where cold air settles. Air flows like water, sliding downhill as the sun sets and the air cools, and rising again as it warms after sunrise. As with water, warm air rises and cool air sinks. Downward-flowing air pools in low spots in the landscape, creating sites that freeze earlier and thaw later than sites in adjacent higher areas. Sometimes frost pockets are obvious depressions. At other times, they are simply pools of dead air that gather downwind of an obstacle that inhibits airflow. In the same way, a boulder in a river creates a quiet pool immediately below it.

It's easy to see the major topographic features of the Rocky Mountain region: the peaks that pierce the sky, the ridges that ripple the prairie, the valleys that slice the hills. Reading the microtopography of your yard—an undulation here or a bump there, the shapes that channel airflow like water in a stream—involves gardening detection: training your eye to "see" like a plant.

Start by looking at the surrounding landscape to visualize channels and patterns of air movement. Are there nearby ridges that air rushes up and over? Trees to slow the aerial current? Do you live at the mouth of a valley, a natural channel for air? Scan your yard, tuning your perception to small undulations, indentations, and obstacles to airflow. Sit or lie on the ground in different locations to feel what the air movement and temperature is like at soil level. Before you know it, you'll begin to think like a plant.

It's Too Steep!

If your site is on a slope that's too steep to garden, one option is to take a cue from the terraced hills and mountainsides found in mountain ranges from the Himalayas to the Andes and carve a series of level, steplike garden spots into the slope.

The idea is simple: dig into the slope and use the fill to create a level terrace or apron, then move up- or downhill to create the next terrace. A retaining wall of rock, railroad ties, or landscape timbers anchored to the slope prevents the terrace from eroding. Dry-laid walls allow moisture to drain downhill; mortared walls must include weep holes for drainage or the weight of the water dammed up in the soil will eventually topple them.

Depending on your overall garden design, terraces can be uniformly sized and spaced, like stair steps, or they can be irregular, with undulating borders that follow the shape of the slope. Steps of rock, flagstone, cement, or timbers can ramble up the slope to connect the terraces. Landscape bare slopes between terraces with hardy, low-care species that will hold the soil against erosion. (See "Plants for Any Zone in the Rockies" on page 15 for suggestions.)

Designing in Place

Gardeners have been working with difficult sites for as long as they've been planting. Quirks are what give any yard character and make it special, and they stimulate creativity. That low spot that fills with water every spring, for instance, might be the perfect spot for a garden pond or bog, and the stubborn rock outcrop could be just the place to grow alpine plants.

A site plan maps the big picture of your garden environment, highlights its unique features, and guides decisions on where and what you'll plant. Drawing a site plan gives you a clear picture of your landscape, warts and all. A site plan doesn't have to be fancy. Start with a sheet of graph paper (an 11- by 14-inch page will give you more space for detail), a ruler, and measuring tape (a 100-foot tape is best). First draw in the permanent stuff: buildings, driveways and walks, and topographic features including boulders and drainage areas. Sketch topographic lines to indicate contours. Mark north so you can calculate solar angles in winter; map airflow, including the direction of prevailing winds and frost pockets; and note soil conditions such as where the soil is thin or sandy or where it's full of construction junk.

It's Too Flat!

Unlike slopes, flat sites may not drain at all. One option is to create drainage by constructing a dry stream channel. Dig a trench in the soil, giving it some curves like a real stream. Begin with a shallow trench near the area you want to drain and gradually deepen it so that its bottom slopes enough to drain water away. Fill the trench with cobbles, then landscape with rounded boulders and streamside plants.

Another option is to create a small pond, either in the low spot itself or in another area, with a stream channel leading to it. Dig out the low area, line it with pond liner, and then landscape with pond or marsh plants, turning a problem into a garden feature.

Flat sites can also be monotonous. Constructing a berm—a linear mound that simulates the hill and ridge shapes of a native landscape—is one way to add topography and interest. A berm several feet high with plants on top of it can lend privacy to an otherwise public front yard or shelter a small patio.

To determine the height and shape of a berm, first decide on its purpose. Is it just to add interest, or must it shield your view of passing traffic or a neighbor's house? What sort of plants will it hold?

Next, test your site before building the berm. To judge the berm's screening effect, run a string between two posts or trees at its approximate height, adding the height of mature plantings. Look over the string from various angles, both while seated and standing. Trace the outline of the berm on the ground with spray paint to check shape and extent. Alter if necessary. Curving berms are usually the most aesthetically pleasing.

Berms can also serve as water-retention devices. Plants on the upstream side of a berm receive more natural runoff than those on the downstream side. Do not place a berm where it will direct or capture water near foundations or patios.

Why Grow Rocks?

Rocks are a fact of life in this region. There's a reason it's called the Rocky Mountains! Rather than attempting to remove every rock, consider incorporating rocks into your garden; in other words, if you can't beat 'em, join 'em. A boulder lends natural character to your garden, creating a focal point for a bench or tall grouping of plants. Boulders also supply topographic relief to a flat site, and they shade plants that suffer from too much sun. A grouping of several smaller boulders forms a natural garden sculpture and provides a site for a rock garden or alpine plants. Best of all, boulders are the ultimate in easy-care landscaping. They never need watering, fertilizing, or trimming; they last forever; and they provide interesting colors and textures. Boulders may come with a beautiful tapestry of lichen and moss—a bonus miniature garden. Native rocks blend with the surrounding landscape, anchoring the garden in place.

Smaller rocks make great mulch. They shade the soil and prevent moisture from evaporating from it, a definite plus in our arid region. Many native plants thrive best with a thin layer, no more than one-half inch deep, of crushed gravel on the soil surface, which not only protects the soil but also provides the ideal germinating medium for seeds.

Use river rock or cobbles (rounded rocks three- to six-inches in diameter) to form dry streambeds on flat landscapes, creating interest while solving drainage problems. Cobbles laid on the surface can edge informal beds. They also can provide a natural surface between beds that keeps the soil moist and acts as a deer deterrent, since these hoofed browsers avoid surfaces that make for unstable footing.

Plants for Any Zone in the Rockies

Flowers

Antennaria parvifolia (pussy-toes) – A slow-growing native that produces mats of small, silvery green leaves; great for stabilizing dry banks and filling between paving stones; low allergy. Blooms from June to September; Zones 3–7.

Gaillardia grandiflora 'Goblin' (Goblin blanket flower) – A long-blooming native with beautiful red and yellow daisylike flowers; fairly drought tolerant but blooms most copiously with regular watering; moderate allergy potential. Blooms from July to October; Zones 3–9.

Narcissus (daffodils) – The hardy single-flowered varieties bloom year after year, multiply with very little water and fertilizer, and are resistant to deer, most rodents, and diseases; insect pollinated and low allergy. Bloom from March to May; Zones 3–9 (depending on variety).

Grasses

Festuca idahoensis (Idaho fescue) – Beautiful blue-green, clump-forming native grass with slender leaves. Lovely accent plant for low borders in combination with blue grama, another native grass. Also forms a tough and erosion-resistant cover for steep slopes on cool aspects. Wind pollinated. Zones 5–10.

Panicum virgatum 'Prairie Sky' (Prairie Sky switch-grass) – Four-foot-tall grass native to the Great Plains with sky blue, upright foliage and sandy colored flower spikes. Great accent plant. Wind pollinated. Zones 4–9 (Zone 3 with winter protection).

Shrubs

Potentilla fruticosa var. *purdomii* 'Forever Gold' (Forever Gold potentilla) – A variety of the native shrubby cinquefoil bred by the Cheyenne Research Center in Wyoming. Cold hardy, somewhat drought tolerant, and covered with small gold flowers all summer. Insect pollinated and low allergy. Zones 2–8.

Rosa (Canadian Explorer and Parkland Series roses,
especially *Rosa* x 'Prairie Joy' and *Rosa* x 'John Cabot.') —
Bred for extremely cold winters and alkaline Rocky
Mountain soils. Prairie Joy resembles a pink-flowering wild
rose and is superb for stabilizing steep banks and forming
low hedges. John Cabot is a vigorous double-flowering
climber. Insect pollinated and low allergy. Zones 3–9.

Trees

Acer platanoides (Norway maple) – A hardy, tall shade tree
that tolerates poor soils and city pollution. Graceful shape;
fall color varies from lemon yellow to butterscotch
depending on variety. Roots may heave pavements.
Needs supplemental water. Plant a female cultivar for allergy prevention. Zones 3–7.

Malus floribunda (crab apple) – Beautiful spring-blooming,
small tree that is hardy and tolerant of a wide variety of
soils. Birds relish the fruits; some fruits make good jelly.
'Radiant' is a sturdy pink-flowering variety; 'Snowflake' is
recommended for its white flowers. Insect pollinated and
low allergy. Blooms May and June; Zones 2–8.

SOIL, GLORIOUS SOIL

*Wherever there are decay and repose, there
begins to be soil. It would be hard to imagine
a more improbable set of ingredients, but even
a truck can become dirt. How can I stand on
the ground every day and not feel its power?*
—William Bryant Logan,
Dirt: the Ecstatic Skin of the Earth

Unless you're planning a hydroponic garden, what you
can grow depends on dirt. Dirt is that stuff underfoot that we
try not to track into the house, that we scrub from our hands
and launder from our clothes. No matter what the dictionary
says, in gardening, dirt is not a synonym for filth. Soil (the
horticulturally correct name for dirt) is a living, breathing
community engaged in the slow process of recycling organic
and inorganic materials into the miraculous substance that
we call dirt. The organic and inorganic compounds in the soil
record Earth's history since life began.

As creatures that walk on the ground, it is understand-
ably difficult for us to conceive what goes on beneath it
because we cannot see what happens there. Millions of
lives—microscopic to macroscopic—have been catalogued
from a square yard of soil: from the frozen DNA of long-
vanished species to plant roots probing sixty feet or deeper.
Dirt is not just a rooting medium; it is alive—a whole
ecosystem unto itself.

In arid climates, the soil provides a much more favorable
environment than the air above ground. Its thermal mass
remains at a relatively constant temperature from day to
night, and it retains moisture more efficiently than air. Where
aridity, heat, or wind stress plant growth, perennial plants
store the bulk of their biomass below the surface, making the
soil a crowded place.

What's My Soil?

Soil scientists classify soils according to an array of characteristics including color and mineral origin. Gardeners should at least know how to determine texture.

Determining whether your soil is sandy, silty, or clayey is pretty simple. Dig a hole a foot or so deep and take a large pinch of soil from several different levels in the hole. Roll each pinch between your fingers while it is dry and note how it feels: Gritty? Smooth? Hard? Lumpy? Loose?

Then dampen each pinch of soil: Does it hold together? Can you squeeze it between your fingers to form a Play-Doh–like ribbon? Or does it crumble and fall apart?

Soil that is predominately sandy feels gritty when dry and wet, and it won't clump even when dampened. Soil that is predominantly silty feels smooth—even silky—when wet, but won't cohere into a ribbon when squeezed. Clayey soil, on the other hand, may be hard and lumpy when dry, but when wet it can be molded just like clay.

Most soils are a combination of these three textures. The predominate texture determines the soil's ability to hold water and nutrients and what kind of environment it provides for plant roots. The relatively large pores in sandy soils don't hold water well and the grains bond nutrients poorly, but the soil's open structure makes a wonderful environment for root growth. Clayey soils are the opposite. The flat clay particles pack tightly, aligning parallel to one another when wet and forming a tight structure difficult for roots to penetrate. Yet clay soils retain water and nutrients better than sandy soils (clay can hold three to six times the water of the same volume of sand). Loamy soils (mostly silt) are intermediate between the two, but are the least common soil texture in our region.

So You've Got ...
Sand or Gravel, Clay, or Construction Junk

The simplest way to handle problem soils, as Lauren Springer writes in *The Undaunted Garden: Planting for Weather-Resilient Beauty*, is to plant native or other species adapted to that particular soil. For sandy soil with low water retention and nutrient levels, pick plants that thrive in sand. In clay soils, with their tendency to expand when wet and harden like cement when dry, use plants adapted to the challenging, but often fertile, soil.

If you can't live with your native soil, one option is to build raised beds and fill them with a mixture of native soil and amendments. Don't forget to loosen the native soil underneath and mix it with the improved soil so that plant roots can penetrate below the raised bed.

Amending native soil without using raised beds is another option. However, don't amend the soil if you're planning to grow natives; they thrive in the soil to which they've adapted over the millennia. Sandy or gravelly soil can be improved by incorporating organic matter, such as compost or well-aged manure. Organic matter helps hold water and supplies the nutrients that sandy soils lack.

Clay's fine texture and small pores can cause plants to experience oxygen deprivation, which can lead to root suffocation. Roots need to breathe too. Adding sand and organic matter to clayey soil helps, but timing is critical. Avoid working these amendments into clay when it's saturated, as the soil compacts and thus loses oxygen. Also avoid working clay when it's dry and hard as rock. Clay is best worked when lightly damp.

Construction wreaks havoc on soil: the topsoil (the thin top layer with organic matter and its community of essential lives) is often scraped off, leaving behind bare mineral soil, containing chunks of concrete and other junk. Tilling in organic matter speeds up the process of rebuilding. But use imported topsoil carefully. Mining it denudes the area it came from, and imported topsoil brings its own complement of seeds and other life-forms, some of which you may not want in your yard.

Who's Underfoot?

Ants, earthworms, millipedes, and comma-shaped, soil-dwelling insect larvae are visible to the naked eye. Yet they're only a small fraction of the multitude of life-forms that inhabit healthy soil. Biologists who study the flora and fauna under-foot estimate that several thousand species—ranging from microscopic microbes to mammals—inhabit Rocky Mountain soils. These include algae, cyanobacteria, protozoa, actinomycetes, fungi, mites, springtails, centipedes, millipedes, spiders, beetles, ants, earthworms, and voles.

These underground legions busily transform bits of organic matter and rock into soil by tunneling, consuming, digesting, and spreading their waste. One species of bacteria, for instance, ingests nutrients from a spider carcass while another breaks the nutrients the first ate into simpler compounds. Then a different bacteria eats the first two species, releasing the nutrients to the soil. Bacteria and fungi are the dominant recyclers of plant and animal tissues.

The result, as Sara Stein writes in *Noah's Garden: Restoring the Ecology of Our Own Backyards,* is that the soil "moves as though on a conveyor belt," constantly churned by the slow but persistent digging of burrowers of all sizes.

Earthworms are the most obvious example of this frenzy of processing and enriching the soil. They do what our mothers told us not to do: eat dirt. Earthworms are crawling tunnelers, ingesting the soil as they tunnel, digesting it with the help of bacteria in their gut, and ejecting it in a trail of nutritious waste. Earthworm castings (excrement) are unbeatable natural fertilizer. They typically contain five times more nitrogen than the surrounding soil, seven times more phosphorus, eleven times more potassium, three times the magnesium, and twice the calcium.

What's pH?

The pH scale measures degrees of acidity and alkalinity. The abbreviation "pH" comes from the German *potenz Hydrogen*, which translates as "power of hydrogen." The scale is based on the ratio of hydrogen ions (which carry a positive charge) to hydroxide, or OH, ions (which are negatively charged).

Neutral pH, where the concentration of positive H ions and negative OH ions are equal, is 7.0. Lower pH values are acidic (higher concentration of H ions); higher pH values are basic, or alkaline (higher concentrations of OH ions). Orange juice is acidic with a pH of 3.0; ocean water is alkaline with a pH of 8.1 to 8.3.

Neutral or near-neutral pH is necessary for many chemical reactions in living systems. The optimum soil pH for plant growth is a slightly acidic 6.4. Most western soils, however, are alkaline, ranging from a pH of 7.0 to 9.0. Peat bogs and other wet, cold soils are the acidic exception with pH values as low as 3.0.

Alkaline soils easily leach mineral nutrients such as iron, manganese, copper, and zinc. Many native plants overcome this deficiency by forming cooperative relationships with soil fungi, exchanging sugars that they produce for the nutrients and water absorbed by the fungal mycorrhizae (threadlike stems that hook into and extend the plant's roots). Regular addition of organic material (compost or well-rotted manure) will gradually lower the pH of alkaline soils.

Tip Garden supply companies sell soil-testing kits; additionally, State Cooperative Extension offices may check soil pH and recommend amendments. Be aware of the source of soil amendments: some synthetic amendments can pollute groundwater by washing out of the soil (nitrates leaching from farm fields in the Midwest, for instance, have polluted wells and are implicated in the occurrence of some types of cancers); some organic amendments, including bat and seabird guano, are mined faster than they can be replaced, robbing the local environment.

It's Too Dry!
It's Too Wet!

Typical soil is about half solid matter and half pore space by volume. Pore space is vital for water and oxygen penetration. A dry soil contains more oxygen than water; a wet soil contains more water than oxygen. Plant root growth occurs most efficiently when no more than half the pore space is occupied by water.

Rocky Mountain soils are usually subject to prolonged seasonal droughts because they are shallow and coarse. Planting native and drought-adapted species makes sense in these soils because that's where they thrive. In fact, too much water or fertilizer shortens their life span.

Mulching the soil surface to retard evaporation greatly improves plant survival in dry soils and reduces the need for irrigation. Effective mulches include landscaping cloth, wood chips or bark, pine needles, grass clippings, and gravel or rock. (See "To Mulch or Not to Mulch," page 46.) Never use plastic sheeting: it does not allow water to penetrate the soil and it prevents the soil from breathing.

Flooded or waterlogged soils are rarely a problem in our

region, except in riparian ecosystems—along streams, rivers, ponds, and marshes or bogs. These soils often contain high levels of organic matter and may be quite deep and fertile, but they are also often waterlogged for all or part of the growing season, posing a very different problem. Their low oxygen levels cause plants to wilt as roots suffocate.

Native riparian plants, including willows, cattails, and marsh marigolds, will thrive in waterlogged soils. Since riparian ecosystems are critical wildlife habitat and also endangered—some 90 percent of the West's riparian ecosystems have been destroyed—it makes sense to leave riparian areas wild or to restore them with native species.

▲ ▼ ▲ ▲ ▼ ▲ ▼ ▲ ▼ ▲ ▼ ▲ ▼ ▲ ▼

SALTY SOILS A white crust on the soil surface and plant leaves that look scorched or withered even when the soil is wet are indications of saline soils. The white crust is excess salt crystallizing when soil moisture evaporates. Naturally salty soils develop from some geologic formations; salts in the soils may also be concentrated by the high evaporation rates in arid climates. Adding organic matter and periodically leaching the soil—watering the soil deeply—to wash the salts below the plants' root zones improves most salty soils.

▲ ▼ ▲ ▲ ▼ ▲ ▼ ▲ ▼ ▲ ▼ ▲ ▼ ▲ ▼

Ants Aren't Bad

A trail of ants marches across your garden on a warm afternoon. Don't reach for the pesticide! Most ants are beneficial to healthy gardens.

Ants' extensive underground nests aerate the soil; their droppings and detritus are an important source of organic matter in arid regions' soils. Ants also pollinate many plant species and distribute their seeds.

Different species of ants play different roles. Some prey on smaller garden insects, others consume and thus clean up detritus including dead insects and spiders, still others gather seeds or farm fungus. A few species milk plant-sucking aphids for their sugary secretions. (See "Outwitting the Invaders," page 88, for tips on minimizing aphid damage.)

Harvester ants are prodigious seed-gatherers. One female worker can haul a seed up to fifty times her weight! Many plant species depend on ants to disperse their seeds because ants often drop their cargo, thus scattering the seeds far from the parent plant. Plants attract their six-legged transport with special handles on the seeds or enticing fragrances.

▲ ▼ ▲ ▲ ▼ ▲ ▼ ▲ ▼ ▲ ▼ ▲ ▼ ▲ ▼

ANT SOCIETY Ants' social organization is among the most complex of any insect. They live in underground colonies as small as several hundred individuals and as large as millions of individuals. Each colony is all female, except during the brief periods when reproductives—fertile, winged females and males—are produced to establish new colonies. All ants in the colony are also all sisters. After mating, a female reproductive breaks off her wings, digs a nest, and lays eggs. (The males die after mating, their purpose accomplished.) As queen of her new colony, she nurtures the first generation of whitish, helpless larvae. Chemical signals from the colony determine whether each larva becomes a worker, foraging for food and tending new generations of larvae, or a soldier, defending the nest and its matriarch.

▲ ▼ ▲ ▲ ▼ ▲ ▼ ▲ ▼ ▲ ▼ ▲ ▼ ▲ ▼

Why Is My Soil So Pale?

Most Rocky Mountain soils lack the deep chocolate brown color of fertile soils that contain high amounts of decayed organic matter. Pale soils develop in dry climates where decomposition is painfully slow. A tree trunk may lie on the forest floor for a century or more before fungi and other decomposers consume it. Moreover, arid environments produce less organic matter to decompose.

Adding compost or well-rotted manure to the soil at least once a year will gradually increase its fertility, improve its texture, and increase its ability to hold water. Watering with compost tea (a brew made by steeping compost in water, throwing away the leached organic matter, and then using the enriched tea) is another way to fertilize pale soils. Unlike when making compost, weeds may be incorporated into the tea without worrying about their seeds germinating in the garden (anything added to the compost pile should be weed-, pest-, and disease-free). However, the liquid tea, while carrying many nutrients, lacks the solid material that improves the soil structure and texture while feeding the soil's flora and fauna.

Chemical fertilizers can cause problems in Rocky Mountain soils. The nutrients in these fertilizers are in the form of easily dissolved and fast-acting salts, which in our arid climate can literally burn or kill the plants if the soil is not immediately watered. Fertilizer salts can also exacerbate salinity problems. Natural fertilizers, including compost and aged manure, are safer for our soils.

Gardening with native or drought-adapted plants sidesteps fertilizer problems. These species are adapted to our region's naturally lean soils and thrive best when soils are not enriched.

Plants for Problem Soils

Sandy Soils

Achillea (yarrow) – A spreading flower with lacy, fernlike leaves
and tightly packed flower heads in colors ranging from pink
and red to yellow and orange. Native species has white
flowers. Extremely cold hardy. Prefers well-drained soils.
Low allergy. Blooms from July to October; Zones 3–9
(depending on variety).

Penstemon barbatus (scarlet buglar penstemon or beardlip
penstemon) – A spring-blooming native wildflower that
sprouts a tall spike of brilliant scarlet flowers. Attracts
hummingbirds. Scarlet buglar penstemon thrives only in
lean soils with infrequent watering. It is a short-lived
perennial but reseeds readily if mulched with gravel
(ants spread the seeds). Low allergy. Zones 4–8.

Ratibida columnifera (Mexican hat or prairie coneflower) –
A prairie native with narrow, divided leaves and yellow or
mahogany flowers shaped like small coneflowers. Blooms
in mid- to late summer. Attracts butterflies. Drought tolerant,
tolerant of limey soils. Low allergy. Zones 4–8.

Clay or Salty Soils

Callirhoe involucrata (wine cup) – A spreading Great Plains
native with spectacular magenta flowers along the length
of the one- to three-foot trailing stems. Long bloomer.
Prefers well-drained soils—too much moisture causes a
bare center. Insect pollinated and low allergy. Blooms from
July to September; Zones 4–9 (3 with winter mulching).

Liatris punctata (prairie gay-feather) – A prairie native that
produces a spike of bright pink-lavender flowers in late
summer. Attracts butterflies. Insect pollinated and low
allergy. Zones 3–8.

Stanleya pinnata (prince's plume) – The native equivalent of wallflower, this clay-loving wildflower sprouts a one- to two-foot-tall stalk of sulfur yellow blossoms. Tolerates somewhat salty soils; rots if soil is wet in winter. Insect pollinated and low allergy. Blooms after snowmelt, May to June; Zones 4–9.

Shrubs

Atriplex canescens (four-wing saltbush) – Native to saline, clayey soils throughout much of the inland West. Shrub three to six feet high and four to eight feet wide with silver-green leaves and tiny, inconspicuous flowers. Drought tolerant, seeds eaten by many birds. Can be sheared into a hedge. Use female plants to prevent allergy problems. Blooms in summer; Zones 3–9.

MICROCLIMATE

The Devil is in the details.
—Popular saying

The USDA Hardiness Zone map shows your yard as Zone 4, but the peonies on the north side of the garden wall froze last winter, while the lavender a few feet away on the south side survived. What's going on?

The peonies were planted in a frigid spot, a microclimate one or more zones colder than the rest of your yard; the lavender on the other side of the same wall inhabits a hot spot where stored solar heat tempers nighttime lows.

Just as the topography of your site (see "What's a Frost Pocket?" page 10) creates warm and cold spots, so, too, do buildings, trees, walls, patios, and solid fencing. By casting dense shade or collecting and radiating solar heat, these features create microclimates (small areas where climatic conditions vary drastically and abruptly).

Areas of dense shade will be cooler and wetter. Less solar radiation equals less heating of the soil surface and thus, less evaporation, resulting in a shorter growing season. On the other hand, areas exposed to intense sunlight, especially next to surfaces that collect solar heat, will be warmer and drier with a longer growing season.

Microclimates are one reason that a plant may thrive in one spot, yet die just a few yards away. Recognizing and understanding the microclimates of your yard is critical to creating a successful and long-lasting garden.

Finding your Microzones

Mapping the microzones or microclimates of your site isn't difficult. Start with your site map (see "Designing in Place," page 12). First, locate the cardinal directions: north, south, east, and west. Then note the placement, size, and shape of buildings, large trees, walls, patios, and other features that cast shade or collect solar heat. These are your yard's microclimates, small areas of differing climate zones.

Using the cardinal directions and the site features, you can roughly figure out areas of sun and shade at varying times of day and times of year. It's easy to see that a tree casts shade, but how does that shade move over the course of the day or the year? How will that shade affect your garden? If you know your latitude and a bit of math, a chart that figures solar angle throughout the year can be helpful in calculating the size and movement of shade and sun. You can find solar angles by searching for "solar angle chart" plus your latitude on the Internet (charts are specific to latitude because the sun's angle changes as you go north from the equator). If you want to plot the specific sun angles of your yard see the directions at http://acre.murdoch.edu.au/refiles /sun/text.html.

Place a thermometer in various yard microclimates and check the temperature at different times of day throughout the year. Charting the temperatures of each spot over time on a piece of graph paper will show you the annual climate variations. With this data and the USDA Hardiness Zone definitions, you can pinpoint your yard's microzones.

▲ ▼ ▲ ▲ ▼ ▲ ▼ ▲ ▼ ▲ ▼ ▲ ▼ ▲ ▼

LIFE IN THE DARK: UNDERSTANDING SHADE
Plants are extremely sensitive to light levels because they make their food using sunlight to drive photosynthesis. Plants growing in inadequate light may produce leggy, weak stems and extra-large leaves in an attempt to increase their photosynthetic surface. If not adapted to shady conditions, a plant may essentially starve to death. One solution is to thin the plant layers and increase the amount of light reaching the ground; another is to plant species adapted to forest understory conditions that will thrive in shade.

▲ ▼ ▲ ▲ ▼ ▲ ▼ ▲ ▼ ▲ ▼ ▲ ▼ ▲ ▼

Desert to Arctic: South Side Versus North Side

The difference between the climate on the south-facing side of a building or wall and that on the north-facing side can be similar to differences in climate hundreds of miles apart. When the sun is at a low angle in the sky, south-facing surfaces collect solar heat. The effectiveness of a surface as a solar collector varies with its physical characteristics: its surface area, the materials it's made from, and what color it is. The larger the surface area and the darker the color, the more heat collected; the denser the material, the more heat stored. Stored solar energy radiates from the surface, heating both air and soil, thus tempering the climate and lengthening the growing season. The air temperature next to a south-facing wall may be thirty degrees warmer than the air temperature next to a north-facing wall.

Since annual plant seeds germinate and perennial plants break dormancy partly in response to soil temperature, a warmer south-facing site means spring arrives sooner. Plants adjacent to a south-facing wall may sprout and bloom a month or more earlier than those adjacent to a north-facing wall (but they may also be more subject to drought and heat stress later in the season).

A north-facing exposure, on the other hand, may be in the shade for half the year, leading to colder air and soil temperatures, shorter day lengths (in botany and horticulture, "day length" is the amount of sunshine the plant receives each day), and thus, a shorter growing season. Plants in these sites break dormancy much later in spring and succumb to frost earlier in fall.

A concrete or stone patio in the sun also functions as a heat sink, absorbing solar energy and releasing it into the surrounding air and soil, effectively creating a warmer and drier microclimate. Concrete readily absorbs water from the soil, adding to the drying effect.

Timing Is Everything: East Versus West

Arid and semiarid climates mean abundant sunshine, because less water vapor in the air results in more cloudless days. In our region (except during the summer thunderstorm season when clouds build for afternoon shade) daytime temperatures are often the highest in late afternoon, after the sun has thoroughly heated the ground. Thus, sites exposed to afternoon sun get scorched, while those receiving sun only in the morning remain relatively mild. Plants on the west-facing side of a house may wilt every afternoon no matter how wet the soil is because they cannot suck enough water into their tissues to retain turgidity, while those on the east-facing side bask in cool shade, and may even grow leggy from insufficient sun.

Changing sun angles throughout the year complicate the east-west dichotomy. West-facing exposures receive the most intense sunlight in summer when the sun is directly overhead. In winter, however, a site that faces north of west will receive much less winter sunlight, while if it faces south of west, it will remain sunny all winter long. Similarly, a site facing south of east will receive more sun in winter than in summer, while a site facing north of east will remain cool and shady much of the year. For cold, shady sites, the best solution is to plant species that will thrive in those conditions.

Tip   **Shade structures, from temporary ones as simple as a piece of cloth stretched between two posts to garden features such as pergolas or overhead trellises, can work wonders on hot, dry sites.**

Designing an Accessible, Safe Garden

Gardeners come in all shapes, sizes, ages, and abilities. Planning gardens that are accessible to all makes gardening easier and more rewarding for everyone.

Pathways at least thirty-six inches wide and gently sloping paths (with grades no greater than 1:12; that is, no more than a one-foot rise or drop in every twelve feet of length) make maneuvering in the garden easier, whether for a wheelchair or a wheelbarrow. Leaving five-foot-radius turnarounds and spaces in front of gates also facilitates wheeled traffic.

Where steps cannot be avoided, build a wide spot at the top and bottom for parking wheeled vehicles. Make sure that the treads on steps are deep and easily visible, and that the risers are a comfortable height for short legs as well as long ones.

When building raised beds, consider making them bench height and wide enough to sit on comfortably. Sitting on the edge of a high bed makes weeding and tending plants enjoyable compared to crouching over or kneeling on a lower bed. Bench-height beds also invite visitors to sit and enjoy your garden.

For safety and ease of use, look for tools with easy-to-grip, padded handles. Keep hoses and other garden accessories out of the way. Label plants and garden chemicals in big letters. Avoid poisonous plants, especially those with attractive flowers, fruit, and foliage that invite picking.

Accommodate garden visitors with limited vision by adding fragrant plants, plants with interesting shapes and textures, and garden features such as waterfalls or fountains that incorporate sounds. The result is a richly rewarding garden that engages all the senses.

Plants for Difficult Microclimates

INTENSE SUN:

Flowers

Lavandula (lavender) – Heat- and drought-tolerant perennial that is native to the Mediterranean region. Fragrant gray-green foliage and spikes of narrow blue or purple flowers. Not cold hardy for the northern Rockies except in protected south-facing locations. Deer proof, low allergy. Blooms from July to September; Zones 5–10 (some varieties only hardy to Zone 6).

Thymus serpyllum (wild thyme) – A ground cover native to the Mediterranean, it is hardy in all but the coldest parts of our region. Perfect for patios and between paving stones. It grows to three inches high and three feet wide with short spikes of purple flowers. Deer proof, low allergy. Blooms in summer; Zones 4–9.

Shrubs

Mahonia repens (creeping mahonia, creeping Oregon grape holly) – Small creeping shrub with hollylike leaves that turn bronze to orange in fall. Clusters of sulfur yellow flowers in spring to early summer are followed by blue berries in fall. Full sun to partial shade; supplemental water required in driest areas. Deer proof, low allergy. Zones 3–7.

Trees

Cercis occidentalis (western redbud) – A small tree native to the foothills of California and the upland Southwest with heart-shaped leaves and magenta pealike flowers that bloom in spring. Leaves turns yellow or red in the fall. Tolerates heat and full sun, needs some supplemental water in driest areas. Insect pollinated, low allergy. Zones 5–10.

SHADE:
Flowers

Arctostaphylos uva-ursi (bearberry, kinnikinnick) – Native
ground cover with small, rounded evergreen leaves. Light
pink urn-shaped flowers in early summer followed by red
berries. Tolerates full sun to full shade, prefers well-drained,
sandy soil. Hardy to Zone 3. Insect pollinated, low allergy.

Heuchera sanguinea (coral bells) – A saxifrage relative that is
native to the southern Rockies with a spike of coral-red
flowers in summer and lovely scalloped basal leaves.
Requires well-drained, humus-rich soil. Deer proof, low
allergy. Zones 4–9.

Hosta (hostas) – One of the classic long-living foliage plants for
shade. Available in a wide variety of leaf textures, shapes,
and shades of green from yellow through chartreuse and
all shades of green to blue; many types of variegation.
Many have spikes of fragrant white or lavender flowers in
summer. Tolerates sun in cool summer climates; requires
enriched soil and some watering. Zones 3–8.

Shrubs

Philadelphus lewisii 'Cheyenne' (Cheyenne Lewis mock orange) –
Another selection of a native shrub by the Cheyenne
Research Center in Wyoming. Early summer bloomer with
fragrant white flowers; grows five to eight feet tall. Insect
pollinated and low allergy. Zones 3–8.

Wild Weather and Changing Climates

DROUGHT and ARID CLIMATES

*If there is magic on this planet,
it is contained in water.*
—Loren Eiseley, *The Immense Journey*

Water in the atmosphere, the minute droplets that precipitate as rain, snow, sleet, hail, or hover as fog, brings the magic of life to our Earth. Scarcity of water renders much of the Rocky Mountain region as arid or semiarid.

A region is defined as arid when the annual precipitation totals are less than the potential evaporation. Aridity means that the environment is drier than it is wet. The intense sun, parched air, and near-constant wind can evaporate significantly more precipitation than falls.

Average annual precipitation across much of the region ranges from less than seven to more than sixteen inches, making it truly arid. The plains along the eastern edge of the Rockies are more accurately defined as semiarid, with annual precipitation amounts averaging fifteen to eighteen inches. Only the higher mountains receive enough precipitation to avoid being labeled arid.

Drought (long periods of time without rainfall or when precipitation is scant) is normal in arid and semiarid climates. In Colorado, for instance, climate records show the state has weathered six drought cycles since recordkeeping began in 1893. Thirty-six of the past 109 years were dry ones, an average of one droughty year in every three.

Plants adapt to aridity in many ways. Annual plants sprout, grow, and reproduce only when moisture is abundant. Perennial plants depend on water-conserving strategies including storing water in their tissues, shading their leaf surfaces, and even dropping their leaves altogether.

▲ ▼ ▲ ▲ ▼ ▲ ▼ ▲ ▼ ▲ ▼ ▲ ▼ ▲ ▼

WHAT'S NORMAL PRECIPITATION? The lower the average precipitation, the more normal a wide variation from year to year. Thus, where the average annual precipitation totals nine inches, it is just as normal to receive five inches in a year as it is to receive twelve.

Some average annual precipitation amounts for the region:

Albuquerque, New Mexico	8.9 inches
Aspen, Colorado	16.5 inches
Billings, Montana	15.1 inches
Boise, Idaho	12.1 inches
Calgary, Alberta	15.7 inches
Cheyenne, Wyoming	14.4 inches
Denver, Colorado	15.4 inches
Fort Collins, Colorado	14.2 inches
Jackson, Wyoming	17.2 inches
Missoula, Montana	13.5 inches
Vail, Colorado	30.0 inches

▲ ▼ ▲ ▲ ▼ ▲ ▼ ▲ ▼ ▲ ▼ ▲ ▼ ▲ ▼

Surviving with Less Water

In the *Xeriscape Handbook,* Gayle Weinstein notes that knowing when not to water can be more challenging than knowing when to water.

The first rule in watering less seems self-evident: **pay attention.** No matter whether you irrigate manually or with an automatic system, notice where the water goes and avoid wasting water on sidewalks, driveways, and other hard surfaces. Keep your irrigation systems in good repair: a leak of 100 drops per hour equals 350 gallons of water lost per month. Check soil moisture before and after watering (see below).

Be flexible. Timers and automatic systems are great, but they lack the ability to compensate for the weather. Get a rain gauge and notice how much precipitation you've received in a given week; adjust your irrigation accordingly.

Timing is critical. During the hot months, water in the early morning and evening when the air is calm and relatively cool. Sprinkler systems can lose 40 to 50 percent of the water to evaporation during the day. In winter, irrigate during the warmest parts of the day. (Plants need moisture year-round, especially during dry and windy winters.)

Deliver water slowly. Sprinkler systems are popular for lawns, but their water delivery efficiency is only 65 to 75 percent because some of their spray evaporates directly into the air. Use soaker hoses or drip systems wherever possible: they deliver water directly to the soil and lose very little to evaporation.

Tip   **To test soil moisture, thrust a flat-bladed screwdriver into the soil as far as it will go. If it is easy to push, the soil is moist; in dry soil, the blade will only penetrate with difficulty. If the blade comes out with pieces of soil clinging to it, press them between your fingers: if they stick in gummy clumps or ribbons, the soil is saturated.**

How Much Water Does Your Lawn Need?

Lawns use the most water in home landscapes, in part because grasses have shallow roots and because we plant thirsty grass species. Experts estimate that lawn irrigation uses as much as 60 percent of the West's urban water.

How much water your lawn requires depends on the type of grass you have, as well as on the soil and your local climate. Lawns on sandy soils, for instance, may require more water since these soils don't hold moisture. In climates with spring and summer precipitation, the amount of natural moisture directly reduces lawn irrigation needs.

Cool-season lawn grasses (those that green up early in the spring), including Kentucky bluegrass, tall fescue, and perennial ryegrass, are generally native to wetter climates and thus are water hogs. Kentucky bluegrass comes from rainy Britain and northern Europe, and guzzles eighteen gallons of water per square foot each year. Crested wheatgrass is the exception. It is a drought-tolerant, cool-season grass native to arid Eurasia. However, its tough stems are not the best texture for a mowed lawn.

Warm-season grasses, those that green up in late spring and early summer, are much less thirsty. They use as little as one-sixth the water required by Kentucky bluegrass. Cultivars of native blue grama and buffalo grass thrive as lawns over most of the region. Buffalo grass, however, will not survive above 7,500 feet elevation. Warm-season grasses require less mowing and fertilizing.

▲ ▼ ▲ ▲ ▼ ▲ ▼ ▲ ▼ ▲ ▼ ▲ ▼ ▲ ▼

WATER DEMAND FOR DIFFERENT LAWNS

Cool-season grasses

Kentucky bluegrass	2 inches/week (hot weather)
Fescues	1 inch/week minimum
Ryegrass	1 inch/week minimum
Warm-season grasses	1 to 1.5 inches/3 weeks (hot weather)
Crested wheatgrass	1 to 1.5 inches/3 weeks (hot weather)

▲ ▼ ▲ ▲ ▼ ▲ ▼ ▲ ▼ ▲ ▼ ▲ ▼ ▲ ▼

Measure-to-Measure: Efficient Watering

Wise water use is the key to maintaining a beautiful yard and garden. To calculate efficient use, you'll need to know what type of soil you have (see "What's My Soil?" page 18), the delivery rate of your watering system, and your plants' requirements.

Soils of varying texture absorb water differently. One inch of water penetrates seven inches into sandy soils, but in clay, one inch of water only penetrates four to five inches.

Divide your garden into hydrozones, areas of similar water needs. For example, your lawn would be one zone, your vegetable garden another, and your flower beds still another. The amount of water required by each zone will depend on the soil type, the plants' root depth, and the species' individual water requirements. The roots of most annual plants and lawn grasses don't penetrate more than a few inches, while tree roots are concentrated between a foot and two feet down (but can go much deeper). Perennial and shrub roots normally reach from four to sixteen inches below the surface. Water only to the plants' rooting depth.

Next, measure your watering system's delivery rate. Place half a dozen empty cans of the same size around your yard, run the watering system for half an hour, and then measure the water depth in the various cans. Multiply the water depth in each can by two for the hourly rate of water delivery.

Now use the data to determine water needs for each hydrozone. For example, if your system delivers an inch per hour to a vegetable garden on sandy soil, half an hour of watering will wet the soil to about six inches deep, just right for the root zone. The cans tell you how much water your system delivers; use a screwdriver to check for penetration.

Tip   **Group plants according to their water needs. Don't plant a species that guzzles water next to one that prefers dry "feet," or it will get root rot.**

What to Do with Too Much Lawn

What if you could shrink your lawn and replace portions of it with surfaces that never needed watering, weeding, fertilizing, or mowing? You can, by using what landscapers call hardscape (patios, decks, paths, boulders, and other low-maintenance surfaces).

First, think about how you use your yard. Imagine it as a series of outdoor rooms. What rooms do you use the most? How do you use them? Which ones do you use least?

Front yards, for instance, are typically used very little because they are open to the street. Structures such as fences, walls, or berms planted with screening plants can turn a front yard into a private space, expanding your options. Replacing the lawn with a deck or patio transforms a high-maintenance lawn into easy-care space for relaxing and entertaining—if it's private enough.

Backyards are the workhorses of home landscapes, where we normally do most of our outdoor living. Here, lawns make the most sense, but are most effective close to the house where they can provide a cool island of green that invites outdoor activities. Consider replacing some of your back lawn with patios or decks, paths of crushed gravel or rock, boulders, or dry stream channels to direct water from your roof to plantings. Expand flower beds to replace high-maintenance, high-water-use turf.

Lawn grasses don't grow well in the shade of trees, and their dense network of shallow roots robs water and nutrients from deeper tree roots. Removing lawn under the canopy of large shade trees and replacing it with a layer of bark or rock mulch is one easy way to improve tree health and reduce lawn area.

Tip **Landscape designers often plan areas of hardscape equal in size to the planted areas of a yard.**

▲ ▽ ▲ ▲ ▽ ▲ ▽ ▲ ▽ ▲ ▽ ▲ ▲ ▽ ▲ ▽

EDIBLE LANDSCAPING Food gardens have traditionally been segregated from ornamental landscaping, but they don't need to be. Many food plants are decorative and make delicious additions to landscaping. If you're removing lawn, why not replace some of it with vegetables and fruits? Rhubarb, for instance, makes a striking (and also pest-resistant) accent plant in a perennial bed, with its large leaves and red stalks. An annual bed artfully planted with tomatoes, eggplants, and summer squash, and edged with different kinds of basil, lettuce, or parsley is quite ornamental. The foliage of lettuce, chard, and spinach makes a beautiful and edible display; strawberries are a yummy ground cover. And don't forget about the wonderful dual-purpose plants—edible flowers. Among the most common and tasty are tulips, roses, nasturtiums, pansies, Johnny jump-ups, calendulas, scarlet runner beans, chives, rosemary, and basil. If you are going to eat flowers, make sure they have been grown organically. Do not eat flowers from nurseries or florists.

▲ ▽ ▲ ▲ ▽ ▲ ▽ ▲ ▽ ▲ ▽ ▲ ▽ ▲ ▽

Tough Love:
More Water Is Not Better

Gardeners are more likely to kill plants by overwatering than by underwatering. That's not surprising: we cannot see the effects of saturating the soil. Plant roots need to breathe (exhale carbon dioxide and inhale oxygen). Saturating the soil's pores with water drives out the oxygen, potentially suffocating plants' roots. Plants grow roots most efficiently where no more than half the soil's pores hold water.

Watering less often and more deeply is better for plant health: it encourages roots to grow deeper. Plants with roots located below the quickly drying soil surface are more drought resistant. Roots only grow in moist soil: they avoid dry areas and die back when the soil dries out. The roots with the greatest number of fine hairs (the structures that take up most of the water and minerals) are usually concentrated in the top six inches of the soil.

Too much water is the death knell for plants native to arid and semiarid ecosystems: they grow leggy and floppy, and quickly succumb to root or crown rot.

WHAT'S A NATIVE? The word *native* is sometimes used in confusing ways. A native species is simply one that occurs naturally in a particular area. Every plant is native to somewhere. Crocus, for instance, is native to Asia Minor, not to North America. *Wildflower* is another term that is used loosely. Many seed mixes labeled "wildflower mix" actually contain nonnative plants or plants native to other regions. Some even contain noxious weeds! Read the species' lists on seed mixes carefully so you know what you're planting.

Just because a plant is native to a region does not mean it will thrive everywhere in that region. Plants grow best in conditions similar to their native ecosystems. Thus, a plant from moist, shady mountain forests may die in a sunny, low-elevation garden.

Xeriscaping Is Not "Zero-Scaping"

In the 1970s the Denver Water Board coined the term *xeriscaping*—a combination of *xeric*, Greek for "dry," and *landscaping*—to describe water-thrifty landscaping. Xeriscaping simply means landscaping designed to use less water.

Xeriscaping is based on common sense. "Why, as gardeners, should we torture ourselves, growing plants from radically different climates?" writes Rob Proctor in the *Xeriscape Plant Guide.* The answer, he says, is to grow plants that thrive in our region.

Selecting appropriate plants for a site is one of the guiding principles of xeriscaping. Other principles include integrating efficient irrigation and maintenance into the planning; reducing high-water-use areas, including lawns; using ecologically sensible methods of soil amendment; mulching the soil; and employing other environmentally sound practices. In sum, xeriscaping is environmentally friendly landscaping that uses water efficiently and is appropriate to the site and region.

Xeriscapes can be as lush as a mountain meadow in full bloom or as spare as a desert during a drought. The key to successful xeriscaping is working with the natural characteristics of the site and plant species appropriate not only to the climate, but also to the native ecosystems. If you live in a sagebrush shrubland, for instance, select species appropriate to a shrubland, not to a spruce forest.

At the heart of the xeriscape concept is the idea of honoring the character and spirit of the landscape where you garden and not trying to force your site to be unnatural.

My Trees Are Turning Brown

Drought conditions are especially hard on large plants such as trees. Plants are essentially water columns: they pull water in from the soil through their roots and transpire it into the air through pores in their leaves. In between, water inches up the narrow tubes of xylem (special circulatory cells), pulled by capillary action, then trickles down in phloem cells, bearing the carbohydrates produced in photosynthesis.

When soils dry out and plants can no longer pull water into their roots, plants' circulatory systems fail and photosynthesis ceases. It's easy to see the signs of drought stress in small plants: they wilt. With trees and shrubs, watch for browning at the leaf edges or needle tips. With continued drought, leaves or needles simply drop off.

Water trees and shrubs whenever conditions are dry, including during warm spells in winter. Be sure to water the entire area under the canopy, since roots extend underground at least as far as the canopy spread. Where landscape watering is banned, hand water with soaker hoses or deep-root tools.

Tip
The rule of thumb for tree watering is ten gallons of water for each diameter-inch of the tree. Thus, a four-inch diameter tree requires forty gallons of water per watering—once a week in severe droughts for established trees (newly planted trees might require watering every day).

▲ ▼ ▲ ▲ ▼ ▲ ▼ ▲ ▼ ▲ ▼ ▲ ▼ ▲ ▼

SUNBURN! Plants sunburn just as people do. The cloudless days of arid climates equal greater exposure to sunlight; high elevations bring greater doses of UV radiation. Both can cause sunscald in plants. Leaves brown or bleach, fruit develops withered spots, or bark splits and dies. New transplants are at greatest risk. Protect tender plants with sunshades, burlap, or shade cloth. Wrap tree bark loosely with tree wrap or strips of burlap.

▲ ▼ ▲ ▲ ▼ ▲ ▼ ▲ ▼ ▲ ▼ ▲ ▼ ▲ ▼

To Mulch or Not to Mulch: Baring It All Is a Bad Idea

Bare soil is the harshest garden environment imaginable. The temperature at the soil surface fluctuates widely from day to night as the sun bakes the unprotected surface during the day. After sunset, the surface chills and the warmth is gone. Water quickly evaporates from the exposed surface, sucking moisture from deeper in the soil, thus drying out the root zone. Bare soil also erodes easily, blown away on the wind or washed away by rain and irrigation.

Mulch is a Rocky Mountain gardener's best friend. Adding a layer of organic or inorganic mulch insulates the soil, tempers oscillations in temperature, and retains moisture. Soil under a thick layer of mulch may be twenty to thirty degrees cooler than nearby bare soil in the hottest parts of the day. Mulch also enriches the soil by making the environment more moderate for the community of soil dwellers, including plants.

Organic mulch, such as wood and bark chips, compost, shredded leaves, pine needles, or dried grass clippings, is most effective when spread three to four inches deep. Keep mulch at least an inch away from tree trunks, stems, and branches to avoid damage from accumulated moisture, and avoid root or crown rot by leaving the crowns of perennial plants uncovered.

Inorganic mulch includes gravel (thin layers are best), cobbles and other rocks, and landscape fabric. Gravel and rock mulches are ideal for many native and drought-adapted plants: they shade the soil surface and retain moisture without promoting crown rot. Avoid using plastic: it is impermeable to both water and gas exchange, and so it kills the soil community. Landscape fabric is not ideal either: wind-blown soil accumulates atop the fabric and under the mulch, making the perfect environment for weed seeds to collect and germinate.

Tip **Mulch annual beds or vegetable gardens in winter by planting a cover crop of grasses or legumes. Be sure to till in the cover crop before it sets seed. Allow several weeks after tilling before planting to allow the organic matter to break down and restore nitrogen levels in the soil.**

No Burn:
Fertilizing Techniques for Arid Climates

Fertilizers provide the minerals that plants need for food production, growth, flowering, and disease and pest resistance. The three minerals often deficient in Rocky Mountain soils are nitrogen (referred to by its chemical symbol, N), phosphorus (P), and potassium (K). Balanced fertilizers deliver all three. Three other major plant nutrients, calcium (Ca), sulfur (S), and magnesium (Mg), are not usually deficient in our soils.

Micronutrients required by plants in trace amounts, include iron (Fe), zinc (Zn), and manganese (Mn). Iron deficiency, which causes one form of chlorosis (a lack of chlorophyll leading to leaf yellowing), is the most common micronutrient problem in Rocky Mountain soils, especially in alkaline or boggy conditions. Iron is necessary to form chlorophyll. Adding chelated iron may solve the problem temporarily, but adding organic matter or sulfur is more effective in the long term.

Chemical fertilizers act quickly because they provide high levels of minerals in a form easily absorbed by plants. Because of these characteristics, however, they easily wash into groundwater and surface water, and they can cause root burn. Root burn occurs because fertilizer raises the concentration of solutes, dissolved particles, in the soil. In dry soils, this causes water to move from the plant roots into the soil by osmosis, thus dehydrating the roots.

The minerals in natural fertilizers are not water soluble; instead, they are released only when broken down by soil microorganisms. Thus, these fertilizers are slower acting, longer lasting, and much less likely to cause root burn or water pollution.

Tip   **Fertilize lawns and gardens in spring, when plants need nutrients most and soils are moist from snowmelt. (Unlike other regions with richer soils, lawns growing in our region's largely nutrient-poor soils need two fertilizations per year, one in spring and one in fall.) Don't fertilize cool-season native grass lawns before they begin growing, however.**

Plants for Dry Times

Grasses

Buchloe dactyloides 'Legacy' (Legacy buffalo grass) – Coarse-bladed, naturally low native grass that tolerates heat, drought, and intense sun. Not shade tolerant and does not survive above about 7,000 feet elevation. Excellent when mixed with blue grama. Plant female cultivars for low allergy. Zones 4–9.

Bouteloua gracilis 'Hatchita' (Hatchita blue grama) – Fine-bladed, bluish green native grass that requires very little water once established, can be mowed as little as twice a season. Does not do well with heavy traffic, such as on soccer fields, but is ideal for home lawns, especially when blended with buffalo grass. Plant female cultivars for low allergy. Zones 3–10.

Flowers

Ceratoides lanata (winterfat) – A small shrub with beautiful silvery leaves and fuzzy silver flower heads in summer. Native to the arid inland West; tolerates clayey and salty soils. Long lived; a good silvery accent in the garden. Plant female cultivar for low allergy. Zones 3–7.

Hemerocallis (daylilies) – These tough perennials native to Asia are hardy to Zone 3 and will persist for decades. Flowers of different cultivars range from ivory to yellow and orange to deep rust, with single and double flowers in a range of forms, and single, bi-, or tri-colored blooms from late spring until early fall, depending on the variety. Best in masses. Low allergy.

Tulipa tarda (species tulip) – One of the wild species that modern horticultural tulips were developed from, native to western and central Asia. A small, ground-hugging tulip with starry yellow and white flowers; very drought tolerant; great for naturalizing or letting go "wild" in native grass lawns and rock gardens. Insect pollinated and low allergy. Blooms in May and June; Zones 3–8.

Shrubs

Sabina [formerly *Juniperus*] *scopulorum* (Rocky Mountain juniper) – A medium-height tree with scalelike, blue-green to yellowish evergreen leaves. Birds (especially migrant robins and cedar waxwings) are attracted to its small, blue berries in fall and winter. Tolerates a wide variety of soils; hardy to Zone 3. Plant a female cultivar such as 'Admiral' for low allergy.

Salvia dorrii (Great Basin sage) – This fragrant shrub with blue-purple flowers in summer is in the mint family, unlike sagebrush, which is in the sunflower family. Native to the high desert from Washington to northern Arizona, it grows one to three feet high and up to four feet wide. Insect pollinated and low allergy. Zones 4–9.

FLOOD

And the waters prevailed,
and were increased greatly upon the earth; …
and all the high hills,
that were under the whole heaven,
were covered.
—*Genesis 7:18–22,* the Bible (King James Version)

Flooding, whether from simple overwatering or from rains of biblical proportions, saturates the soil, displacing the oxygen from pore spaces and cutting off the air supply to plant roots. If the soil is not allowed to dry out, plant roots suffocate and eventually die. As the water drains away, oxygen reinfiltrates the pores, and roots begin to breathe again. Plants may survive for quite a while in soils that are soggy but not completely saturated. Low oxygen content weakens plants, makes them susceptible to diseases, causes root rot, and encourages water-mold fungi.

The solution to overwatering is simple: stop watering. Check the soil moisture daily until the soil has dried out. (See "Surviving with Less Water," page 37, for a tip on checking soil moisture.) Measure how much water your sprinkler system is delivering and adjust it to water less frequently or, if it is still flooding the soil, for shorter times. It's better to water longer and less frequently than to water more often for shorter times, however. Watering deeply encourages root growth below the surface of the soil, making plants more drought tolerant.

Surviving natural flooding requires patience: you can't change the weather. Here in the arid West, floods are usually temporary and plants recover. Snowmelt from an especially heavy snow, for instance, may briefly smother plants, but they recover as the soil drains. Temporary flooding can be a blessing, identifying spots in your garden that have poor subsurface drainage. (See "It's Too Flat!" page 12.)

The Soil Is Wet but My Plants Are Droopy

Wilted plants may not need more water. Chronic overwatering not only deprives plants of oxygen, it also washes nutrients out of the soil. Droopy plants growing in moist or wet soil may indicate a lack of nutrients in the soil. They may also indicate the proliferation of any one of various fungi or molds that flourish in wet soils. One drooping plant is probably an isolated condition; a whole area of drooping plants likely indicates a widespread problem.

Check the soil moisture, and if the soil is wet or saturated throughout, let it dry. Inspect the plants for discolored patches or other signs of fungus or rot. (See "Outwitting the Invaders," page 88.) If there is no sign of fungus or mold, take a soil sample for analysis and add the recommended nutrients.

▲ ▼ ▲ ▲ ▼ ▲ ▼ ▲ ▼ ▲ ▼ ▲ ▼ ▲ ▼

DID I KILL IT? Knowing what to do with a struggling plant is sometimes difficult and requires equal parts of ruthlessness and patience. If a plant is diseased and doesn't respond to treatment, it's usually best to haul it out of your garden before it infects other plants. But if it shows no signs of disease, give it some time. Try changing your management regimen: adjust the watering, mulch, and other parameters. Perhaps it's the right plant in the wrong place. Reread its requirements and relocate it to a more appropriate microclimate to give it another chance. If these efforts don't work, cut your losses. Remove the plant and try something else. Remember today's dead plant becomes tomorrow's compost (as long as it is not diseased), which will feed the garden.

▲ ▼ ▲ ▲ ▼ ▲ ▼ ▲ ▼ ▲ ▼ ▲ ▼ ▲ ▼

Burial!

When a stream or river overflows its banks and covers your garden with a layer of bed load (the sediment carried by the water, ranging from boulders to silt) or a flash flood inundates your site with debris, the newly deposited sediment may suffocate your plants.

Don't panic. A thin layer of sediment may be beneficial, delivering much-needed nutrients and enriching your soil. Boulders or cobbles scattered by the flood can add to the beauty of your garden. Surprisingly, your plants may still be alive beneath the new surface. Unless the newly deposited sediment endangers structures, curb your impulse to dig your garden out; instead, wait a season and see what resprouts. You may be surprised: plants are often tougher than we think.

Plants That Survive with Wet Feet

Grasses and grasslike plants

Carex (sedges) – Grasslike plants with leaves that are triangular in cross section. Some species require standing water; others can survive in dry soil. Look for ornamental species with golden and bluish tints or variegated leaves. Wind pollinated. Most bloom in summer; Zones vary with species, from 1–11.

Typha latifolia (cattail) – A three- to six-foot-tall marsh plant with long, narrow leaves and a "hot-dog-on-a-stick" inflorescence, its tightly packed flowers bloom in summer. Prefers permanent surface water, but can survive temporary droughts as long as soil stays moist. Wind pollinated. Zones 3–10.

Flowers

Iris ensata (Japanese iris) – Tall (up to four feet high) iris with flat flowers that appear to float above long leaves. Blossoms range from purple and violet to rose and white. Rhizomes must be in water during growing and flowering season. Low allergy. Blooms in summer; Zones 3–8.

Iris missouriensis (Rocky Mountain iris) – Small iris native to the interior West that form ground-hugging clouds of violet to pale blue blossoms in wet meadows. A tough, cold-hardy, and persistent species that can tolerate dry soils after blooming season. Most eye-catching in masses. Insect pollinated and low allergy. Blooms in June; Zones 3–7.

Shrubs

Swida sericea, formerly *Cornus stolonifera* (Redtwig dogwood) – A native riparian (stream- or riverside) shrub that grows to six or more feet tall. Bright red stems are beautiful in winter; white berries attract birds. Hardy to Zone 3; does not thrive in hot climates. Insect pollinated and low allergy. Blooms June to July.

Trees

Betula glandulosa (bog birch) – Another native riparian shrub
found in the mountains as high as alpine willow bogs.
Grows to five feet tall and nearly as wide with small round
leaves that turn brilliant orange to deep maroon in fall.
Zones 2–6.

Picea pungens (Colorado blue spruce) – Tall native evergreen.
A stately tree for large spaces, subject to gall-forming
aphid infestations and to being easily uprooted in strong
winds. Wind pollinated. Zones 2–6.

CLIMATE CHANGE

All we really know is that the weather
is going to be different than it has been
in the past. Unheralded species of plants,
waiting in the wings like Broadway
understudies, may become dominant
over time, while old favorites decline.
From the garden where I work,
the plants seem to be telling us
something we may not want to hear:
the world is changing.

—Peter Del Tredici,
"A Camellia Grows in Boston,"
New York Times, 26 November 2002

The USDA Plant Hardiness Zone map, garden books,
plant and seed catalogs, and the labels on the plants you buy
all give information on climate and what plants will survive
where. There's one large problem with this information
though: it's all based on the past, which may no longer be
a good predictor of the future.

For several decades scientists have been warning with increasing alarm that levels of carbon dioxide in the atmosphere are rising more rapidly than is normal. Increased levels of this gas—called greenhouse gas because it traps and reflects incoming solar heat like the glass in a greenhouse—are raising global temperatures, creating a phenomenon dubbed global warming. The global warming theory is controversial. Everyone from scientists to politicians has weighed in on its validity.

But the data are increasingly difficult to ignore: the World Meteorological Organization, an apolitical body of the United Nations, notes that monthly and annual average temperatures around the globe have been increasing gradually for the past one hundred years. The rise in Northern Hemisphere temperatures during the twentieth century, in fact, may be the largest rise in any century in the past one thousand years.

The rise in global temperatures is already reflected in altered distributions of animals and plants. In Colorado, pikas, the high-mountain rabbit relatives that whistle from rockslides, have recently disappeared from seven of twenty-five sites where they were once plentiful as high-mountain habitat warms and dries out. On the Great Plains, blue grama grass, a cool-season native grass that does not grow well when nighttime temperatures rise, has declined over twenty-three years of warmer average temperature. At the Arnold Arboretum in Boston, tender species such as camellias, never successfully grown outside the greenhouse, now thrive outdoors.

▲ ▼ ▲ ▲ ▼ ▲ ▼ ▲ ▼ ▲ ▼ ▲ ▼ ▲ ▼

ZONE SHIFT What does global warming mean for gardeners? That's not entirely clear. If average temperatures continue to rise, species adapted to warmer climes may expand northward and at higher elevations, while species adapted to colder climes may grow increasingly scarce or disappear. Places that once were a Zone 3 may warm to Zone 4 or perhaps even Zone 5, equivalent to a move from Calgary to Denver. (The USDA has revised the Plant Hardiness Zone map in an attempt to reflect these changes; however, many experts consider the new map preliminary since the effects of global warming are not easy to predict.) Even if average precipitation remains constant, warmer temperatures will raise evaporation and transpiration rates, meaning that soils will dry out more quickly and less water will be available to plants.

▲ ▼ ▲ ▲ ▼ ▲ ▼ ▲ ▼ ▲ ▼ ▲ ▼ ▲ ▼

Warmer air temperatures and higher evaporation rates also mean warmer soil temperatures. Plants are extremely sensitive to soil temperature. It is one of the main cues for root growth and transpiration. Plant roots die when soil temperatures become unfavorable.

Species at the southern margins or lower elevations of their range are likely to struggle or die as climates warm, while species adapted to heat and drought will flourish. For example, you may be desperately trying to save your blue spruce trees while your cactus thrive.

If the Globe Is Warming, Why Is It So Cold This Winter?

Although the global warming theory is so called because of its predictions of rising global temperatures, the heart of the theory is less about warming than about unpredictability. As the globe heats due to climate change, the number and intensity of what meteorologists call extreme weather events are expected to increase.

That means more severe weather, cold as well as hot, rain as well as drought, more tornadoes, hurricanes, cyclones, blizzards, and torrential rains.

The year 2002, for example, was a record drought year across much of the Rocky Mountain region. Meager winter snows, above average temperatures, and insufficient summer rains combined to deliver less than half the average annual precipitation in some places. It was drier than some of the worst droughts of the late 1800s, dry enough to be ranked as a three-hundred-year drought in some areas.

In 2003, March brought a record blizzard to a portion of Colorado's Front Range, paralyzing the Denver metropolitan area with four to eight feet of snow. May shattered another record when 562 tornadoes, the most ever recorded by far in any single month, tore through the Great Plains and the Southeast.

El Niño: How Can the Ocean Affect My Garden?

The Rocky Mountains may seem to be a long way from the Pacific Ocean, but our region is intimately connected to that great body of salt water. Storms that form over the Pacific, blown eastward by high-altitude jet streams, supply much of our winter moisture.

The amount of moisture reaching western North America from the Pacific each year depends on complicated interactions between short- and long-term oscillations in ocean levels and surface water temperatures which scientists have only begun to identify.

How can ocean surface temperature shifts affect precipitation thousands of miles away? Warm water at the ocean's surface evaporates more easily than cool water, thus seeding the westerly jet streams with more moisture-bearing storms. In addition, warm surface water moves around in the Pacific, pushed by trade winds and displaced by cold, nutrient-laden upwellings that nurture fisheries along continental coasts.

When Pacific trade winds quit blowing, they trigger a short-term oscillation in southern Pacific surface temperatures and levels, allowing warm water to accumulate and actually raise sea levels along the South and Central American coasts. This condition, dubbed El Niño (Spanish for "the Christ Child," since it appears around Christmas time), generates increased precipitation from Peru to the American Southwest. When trade winds revive, warm surface water is pushed back to the western Pacific, lowering sea levels and returning the cool upwelling to the South American coast and precipitation to Indonesia and Australia.

The Pacific Decadal Oscillation (PDO), a newly described, several-decades-long switch in northern Pacific Ocean temperatures and surface levels, complicates the El Niño pattern. In the negative phase, a horseshoe-shaped mass of higher-than-normal ocean temperatures and ocean levels forms in the western Pacific, leaving a wedge of lower-than-normal ocean temperatures and ocean heights along the coasts of North and Central America. This diverts the jet stream north, resulting in dry and warm winters for the Rockies and American Southwest.

In the positive phase, the higher-than-average ocean temperatures and levels switch to the eastern Pacific, bringing above-average moisture for western North America.

The most recent positive or wetter-than-normal phase ran from 1977 to 1999. The year 2000 ushered in a new phase: several decades of drier-than-normal western weather.

Plants for Warming Climates

Flowers

Echinacea purpurea (purple coneflower) – Medium to tall perennial with large purple flowers. Great in wild plantings or toward the middle or back of the border in more formal gardens. Great Plains and Rocky Mountain native. May cause respiratory allergies. Blooms August to September; Zones 4–9.

*Eschscholzia californica (*California poppy) – Native to the dry grasslands of the California coast ranges, this lovely annual with orange flowers over blue-green, ferny foliage flourishes in dry soils during hot summers. It self-sows, so it is best in informal plantings. Insect pollinated and low allergy. Blooms all year long if the weather is mild and the soil moist. Annual.

Linum perenne var. *lewisii* (blue or Lewis's flax) – Short-lived, airy perennial with round, sky blue flowers that open each morning and close in the heat of the day. Self-sows, so plant in large masses or informal plantings. Heat and drought tolerant. Named for Meriwether Lewis of the legendary Lewis and Clark expedition. Insect pollinated and low allergy. Blooms from June to September; Zones 3–9.

Shrubs

Juniperus horizontalis (spreading juniper) – An evergreen shrub that tolerates warm, dry soils. True to its name, this hardy native spreads up to six feet wide rather than growing more than a few feet tall, and its tiny, scalelike leaves are not prickly like other shrub junipers. A great choice for hot, dry, difficult sites. Plant female cultivars to prevent allergy problems. Zones 5–8.

Yucca glauca (narrowleaf or plains yucca) – With two-foot-long evergreen leaves forming a spiky rosette and a several-foot-tall spike of waxy ivory flowers in spring, this drought- and heat-tolerant native member of the lily family makes a great accent plant. Don't plant it where its awl-tipped leaves can injure passersby. Moth pollinated and low allergy. Zones 4–7.

Trees

Catalpa speciosa (western catalpa) – Hardy to Zone 3 and reaching sixty feet tall in good conditions, this native western shade tree sports huge, heart-shaped leaves and frilly white flowers in spring, followed by long, bean-shaped pods in summer. A spectacular shade tree that is relatively drought tolerant once established.

EXTREME WEATHER

*"If you don't like the weather,
wait a minute."*
—Popular saying

Rocky Mountain weather is rarely calm. Weather in arid climates tends to be changeable because dryness and air movement go hand in hand: the drier the landmass, the less it buffers temperature changes between day and night. The greater the diurnal temperature changes, the more active the air movement. As the ground heats up during the day, reflected solar radiation warms the air next to the ground, generating spiraling upcurrents or thermals. Thermals add turbulence and speed to local air movement, increasing breezes to gusts.

In addition to aridity, the region's topography is as rumpled as a bedspread after a difficult night. Air flows across the jumbled landforms the way water flows in a creek channel: seeking the easiest course, speeding up when the landscape gradient steepens, slowing down as it flattens. Like water, air creates waves, which can be as turbulent as any rapids on the downstream side of obstacles such as ridges and peaks.

Around high peaks and ridges, the very landscape seems to breathe. Air around the peaks warms and rises when the sun hits the high country, drawing up cool air from below to replace the warmed air above. In the evening, as the sun sets, the air up high cools quickly and flows downhill.

Add moisture to moving air and rumpled topography and what you get is weather so changeable, and sometimes so violent, that it lends truth to the old Chinese curse, "May you have an interesting life."

Blizzard!

Snowfall has been recorded in some part of the Rocky Mountain region for every month on the calendar. According to meteorologist and author Richard A. Keen, at the region's generally high elevations, any cloud big enough to precipitate is probably also tall enough that its top is well below freezing. Even summer rains begin as hail in freezing cloud tops, and only melt into liquid as they fall through gradually warming air.

Snowfall is usually a boon to gardens, insulating the soil from freezing temperatures and providing crucial moisture. Meltwater from accumulated snowpack provides the region's water, filling streams, rivers, and reservoirs, and seeping into the soil to recharge groundwater.

In the northernmost portions of the region and at the highest elevations, Pacific storms delivering snow make winter the wettest season. On the plains and in much of the rest of the region, moisture sweeping north from the Gulf of Mexico in spring combines with Pacific moisture to make spring the soggiest season. Only the very southernmost edge of the Rocky Mountain region doesn't depend on snow for the bulk of its annual moisture; its moisture comes as rain from the Southwest's summer monsoons.

When snow comes as blizzards dumping unusually large amounts of precipitation, it can wreak havoc on gardens. The sheer weight of wet spring snows can topple or break tree branches, smash shrubs, and smother smaller plants—not to mention collapse porches, carports, and roofs. The wettest snows usually come in spring, when the relatively warm air can hold more water, thus forming larger, wetter snowflakes.

Snow Loads and Plant Architecture

Just as buildings in snowy climates are designed to carry large snow loads, plants adapted to those climates have features that allow them to avoid snow damage: they either leaf out late to avoid accumulating snow and thus broken branches or have leaves or needles with small surface areas to shed snow.

To minimize spring blizzard damage, don't plant annuals or fragile plants until after snow season has passed or the date of the last frost. Select perennial plants with snow-shedding architecture (form, branching pattern, and leaf shape) to weather heavy snow loads. Think of how buildings behave with heavy snow loads: flat roofs often collapse under deep snow, but snow slides off steeply pitched roofs. Weeping plants such as weeping cherry trees and plants with long horizontal branches suffer the same problems as flat roofs: they collapse under heavy loads. Similarly, trees and shrubs that leaf out early can collect enough snow on the canopy to overload and collapse the branches.

Choose trees and shrubs with small leaf surfaces rather than large, and select plants with leaf surfaces that are nonhorizontal and therefore more likely to shed snow.

Design garden structures with snow loads in mind as well, using forms that shed snow and materials that can withstand accumulated weight. Wet snow is extremely sticky and can adhere to the narrowest of surfaces. A spring blizzard that deposited nearly five feet of wet snow in one mountain valley collapsed rotating clotheslines when several feet of snow piled up on the lines!

Tip **When pruning storm-damaged trees and shrubs, always cut broken limbs back to the tree or shrub trunk. Don't leave a stub, but do leave the collar of bark around the limb intact so that it can grow over the wound. Pruning weak or crossing branches before a storm will limit damage.**

It's Freezing Out There!

The length of time between the last hard frost of spring and the first hard frost of fall isn't generous in much of the Rocky Mountain region, especially at high elevations and latitudes.

Frost damage occurs when subfreezing air temperatures affect the water inside a plant's cells; water expands when it goes from liquid to crystal form, bursting cell walls and killing the cells. Plants with an abundance of lush, watery new growth will be more heavily damaged by frost; plants with less new growth will suffer least.

Gardeners can lengthen the short growing season by using protective structures including row covers and water-filled individual plant insulators. Plant the most tender plants in warm microclimates.

Toughening up perennials in late summer will help them survive the coming winter. Stop applications of fertilizer and begin watering less at least six weeks before the average first frost date so that plant growth slows. This allows time for perennial plants to develop a tough cuticle around the newest tissues, giving them some protection against frost and sunburn (plants are more likely to suffer sunburn in winter when their bark dries out).

Tip The dates of the first and last hard frost in any given area will vary from year to year (and may change radically with changing climates). Local microclimates may also cause significant variations even within one general area.

Chart the dates of the first and last hard frosts in your garden each year on a piece of graph paper. The ongoing record will give you an accurate picture of the growing season for your specific location.

▲ ▼ ▲ ▲ ▼ ▲ ▼ ▲ ▼ ▲ ▼ ▲ ▼ ▲ ▼

FALL AND SPRING FROST DATES

September 7—June 1
Calgary, Alberta

September 7—May 15
Butte, Montana
Durango, Colorado
Laramie, Wyoming
McCall, Idaho
Rock Springs, Wyoming

September 23—May 15
Billings, Montana
Bozeman, Montana
Casper, Wyoming
Cheyenne, Wyoming
Fort Collins, Colorado
Helena, Montana

September 28—May 12
Boulder, Colorado
Cedar City, Utah
Denver, Colorado
Idaho Falls, Idaho
Logan, Utah
Mountain Home, Idaho
Pocatello, Idaho
Pueblo, Colorado

October 14—May 1
Boise, Idaho
Grand Junction, Colorado
Moab, Utah
Provo, Utah
Salt Lake City, Utah

▲ ▼ ▲ ▲ ▼ ▲ ▼ ▲ ▼ ▲ ▼ ▲ ▼ ▲ ▼

Big Winds

Aridity and bumpy topography make the Rocky Mountain region a windy place. Regional winds range from relatively innocuous mountain and valley winds—the breezes that blow uphill in the morning and downhill in the evening—to whirlwinds—the trickster spirals that develop from rising thermals on hot days—to powerful Chinooks.

Chinooks, called snow eaters by the Chinook Indians of Oregon, are warm downslope winds that roar out of mountain ranges in winter. Most are westerlies, since the region's winds generally blow from the west. (Salt Lake City's Chinooks are one exception; they blow out of the mountains to the east.) Chinooks begin as lee waves—standing, wavelike ripples that form downwind of a mountain range.

Lee waves can be huge, the air rising and falling a mile or more to flow over crests as far as ten miles apart. Air speeds up as it flows down into the trough between wave crests, like water rushing down a drainage.

Unique lenticular, or lens-shaped, clouds often mark the crest of the wave as moisture in the air condenses. Honed by the rushing wind, these flattened clouds look like spaceships or river-polished stones. Lenticular clouds signal high winds aloft.

In winter, big lee waves may spawn Chinooks with airspeeds of more than one hundred miles per hour. Blowing in relatively warm air from the Pacific Ocean, Chinooks can raise the air temperature tens of degrees in a few minutes: in Spearfish, South Dakota, in January 1943, a Chinook wind hiked the mercury forty-nine degrees in two minutes!

Tip Use windbreaks such as walls, fences, buildings, or rows of thick hedges and trees to shelter
delicate plants. In the Chinook Zone, a band ten to twenty
miles wide along the foothills, avoid planting fast-growing
trees and shrubs that shed limbs easily.

Thunderstorms

Flash! Lightning streaks across the sky followed by the
crash and boom of thunder. It must be summer in the Rocky
Mountain region. All parts of the region experience summer
thunderstorms, but the Sangre de Cristo Range west of Raton,
New Mexico, is the flash and rumble capital of the United
States with an average of 110 thunderstorm days each year.

Cumulonimbus clouds, the tall, anvil-headed clouds that
spawn thunderstorms, form in the unstable air above ridges
and peaks. As the air warms, it streams upward, pulling in air
from all around and developing an updraft. Moisture in the
updraft turns to droplets when it rises past the condensation
point in the air, which is often a sharp line, hence the flat
cloud bottoms "sitting" on the line of condensation.

The latent heat in the vapor is released when the water
condenses, warming the air around it and generating more
updrafts, which pull more moist air into the growing cloud,
eventually pushing its top up past the freezing point. That's
when the cloud changes from a cottony cumulus, or pile
cloud, into a cumulonimbus, or rainy pile, with a freezing
top. Moisture in the freezing top begins to sink, falling as
precipitation.

The powerful updrafts and downdrafts that develop inside
these storm clouds toss the moisture around: snowflakes melt
and fall as rain, and water droplets are sucked back up to
freeze into hail, which can turn garden plants to mush when it
finally hits the ground.

▲ ▼ ▲ ▲ ▼ ▲ ▼ ▲ ▼ ▲ ▼ ▲ ▼ ▲ ▼

LIGHTNING! When supercooled water droplets freeze, electric charges are produced. Air is a poor conductor of electricity, but it cannot buffer the high voltages that cluster at the tops and bottoms of cumulonimbus clouds. Once a leader stroke makes its way from the cloud to the ground, ionizing the air, sparks fly, producing the instantaneous multiple strokes that we perceive as one flash of lightning. The thunder that follows is just the sound of air exploding as it is heated. More than a million cloud-to-ground lightning strikes hit the West each summer.

▲ ▼ ▲ ▲ ▼ ▲ ▼ ▲ ▼ ▲ ▼ ▲ ▼ ▲ ▼

Tip **Summer hailstorms can pummel gardens, flattening plants. Plants native to hailstorm-prone ecosystems often recover quickly; plants with small, fine, less fleshy foliage may avoid hail damage altogether. Row covers on hoops will protect vegetable gardens from both hail and searing midday sun. For especially valuable individual plants, build hail covers of wood frames covered with layers of plastic. Wait a day before pruning hail-damaged plants as some wilting may only be temporary. Water sparingly—too much moisture will make conditions too favorable for tiny grazers and decomposers, causing their populations to explode.**

Weathering Warm, Dry Winters

It appears that cold and snowy Rocky Mountain winters are the norm if you look at an average of the past century or so of climate data. "Average" can be misleading, however. For example, in Colorado, a third of the past 109 years qualify as drought years, with warmer-than-average winter temperatures and lower precipitation. The future may be even warmer and drier. Pacific Decadal Oscillation models predict twenty to thirty years of lower-than-normal precipitation, and global warming theories portend a continuing rise in temperatures.

Since dry air heats and cools quickly, the fluctuation between daytime highs and nighttime lows becomes greater as climates grow more arid. Winter temperatures may oscillate between subfreezing nights and balmy afternoons, tricking plants into breaking dormancy when moisture is limited and making freeze damage likely.

Knowing your garden microclimates and reserving the coolest, moistest spots for the most drought- and heat-sensitive plants will help your garden survive warm, dry winters. Mulch is also critical. Mulch shades the soil surface, keeping it cool and retaining moisture for root survival. Plants growing in bare soil are more likely to break dormancy during the winter, and thus suffer dehydration and freeze damage. Watering during dry winters is essential to keep trees, shrubs, and perennials alive.

Winter watering requires different techniques than those used for summer watering. Instead of watering in the cool, still hours of early morning, as in summer, water on warm days during the warmest part of the day to help avoid frost damage. After watering, drain hoses, faucets, and irrigation systems so that trapped water won't freeze and shatter them.

Tip Pile snow shoveled from walks and driveways on garden beds and in shade tree wells (do not use snow that has salt or deicing compounds in it—these can be toxic to plants). The stored moisture will seep into the soil on warm days, hydrating plant roots.

Plants for Warming Climates

Flowers

Amelanchier alnifolia (serviceberry) – Tall, multi-stemmed shrub or small tree (to twenty feet) with clusters of fragrant white flowers in spring, followed by deep purple berries in mid-summer. Small foliage turns yellow to light red in fall. Extremely cold hardy, it recovers well from hail or snow damage. It is an attractive browse for elk, deer, and moose. Insect pollinated and low allergy. Zones 3–7.

Nepeta siberica (Siberian catmint) – Tall spikes of loose periwinkle blue flowers bloom from early to midsummer, recover well after hail and storm damage, and are very cold hardy. A perennial member of the mint family, easily grown from seed or cuttings. Bee pollinated and low allergy. Zones 3–7.

Penstemon (beardtongue) – A group of native perennials with spikes of tubular flowers ranging from scarlet to blue-purple. Red species attract hummingbirds. Bees pollinate blue to purple species. Frost tolerant, they recover well from hail or snow damage. Bee or hummingbird pollinated and low allergy. Blooms from spring through midsummer, depending on species; Zones from 4–8, depending on species.

Shrubs

Crataegus (hawthorns) – Slow-growing small trees native to
North American and the Asian plains. White (or pink)
flowers in early summer followed by haws (fleshy fruit)
that attracts birds; colorful fall foliage. Small leaves and
strong wood mean minimal snow and hail damage. Insect
pollinated and low allergy. Zones 3–7.

Fallugia paradoxa (Apache plume) – Four- to six-foot-tall native
southwestern shrub with fine, gray-green, long-lasting
foliage, white roselike flowers from spring through summer,
and rosy, Phyllis Diller–hairlike seed heads. Drought tolerant; it prefers lean, dry soil; hardy to -40° F. It recovers well
from hail and storm damage. Insect pollinated and low
allergy. Zones 3–8.

Trees

Picea glauca (white spruce) – Native evergreen tree that grows
to forty feet or more; deep green needles have a whitish
sheen. Fairly drought tolerant once established; strongly
pyramidal form makes it resistant to snow and hail damage; extremely cold hardy. Wind pollinated. Zones 3–6.

WILDFIRE
What's a Fire-Dependent Ecosystem?

Fire is a creation of the living world.
Life created an oxygenated atmosphere,
life created the terrestrial
biomass that burns as fuels.
Combustion simply takes apart what
photosynthesis puts together. …
—Stephen Pyne, "If I Ran the Zoo:
A Survey of Wildland Fire in America"

Summer drought and frequent thunderstorms make fire a natural factor in much of the Rocky Mountain region. Many Rocky Mountain ecosystems require periodic fire to recycle nutrients and regenerate decadent vegetation; such ecosystems are considered fire dependent. In fact, before active fire suppression began, western wildfires were so common that some scientists contend alkaline ash from these fires blown east by prevailing winds may have been an important factor in preventing acidification of eastern lakes and streams.

Tree-ring research shows that before fire suppression efforts, low-intensity ground fires swept through ponderosa pine ecosystems as often as every five or ten years, clearing out small trees and shrubs. This resulted in a savanna of large trees with a grassy understory. Without such periodic fire, today's ponderosa forests are crowded, unhealthy, and dangerously flammable. Similar low-intensity fires burned many lower-elevation ecosystems, including piñon pine, juniper, and limber pine woodlands, oak chaparral, and prairies.

More intense fires are natural in some mountain forest ecosystems. Crown fires, often called "stand replacement" fires because they charred whole stands of trees, occurred on a 150- to 300-year interval in lodgepole pine forests, killing the canopy of trees of similar age, recycling downed material, and preparing the soil for a new generation of lodgepoles. Aspen stands are also dependent on such catastrophic fires, which regenerate aging stands that would otherwise die out.

Periodic fire not only restores soil fertility and rejuvenates vegetation, it also prevents epidemic outbreaks of bark beetles and other organisms by thinning the forest canopy.

Planting and Maintaining a Fire Barrier

The urban-wildland fire interface includes any part of the Rocky Mountain region where fire occurs naturally and dwellings are scattered through wild ecosystems. However, fire-wise landscaping (dubbed "firescaping" in California) and regular maintenance can buffer your home from fire.

Vegetation provides the fuel for fires. But vegetation that is sparse and green burns less well, creating defensible space, an area that naturally slows fire. The three rules of creating defensible space are remove, reduce, and replace. The idea is to create a space with little fuel for the fire to burn.

Remove dead trees and shrubs. Reduce the density of vegetation, both horizontally, by thinning trees and shrubs so they are spaced more widely, and vertically, by trimming up branches so that flames cannot jump from the ground into the crowns of trees. Replace highly flammable vegetation with less flammable plants and nonburnable surfaces. (See page 73 for suggestions.)

With less fuel to combust, flame lengths shorten, fire spread decreases, and fires peter out naturally. When fires reach areas with less fuel, they slow dramatically, drop from tree crowns to the ground, and become easier to control.

Fire-wise landscaping does not mean baring the ground around your house: bare ground dries out surrounding vegetation, raising fire danger, and causes erosion. Instead, use hardscape (driveways, walks, patios, and boulders or rock mulch) to create fire barriers. In addition, grow fire-resistant vegetation—plants with high water content and low flammability. Water features such as ponds and streams can be useful too.

Plants for fire-wise landscaping include low-growing ground covers and shrubs, deciduous trees instead of resin- and oil-impregnated evergreens, vegetable gardens and other well-watered edible landscaping, and even lawns where water is available.

Tip   **Check with your state or provincial forestry service for publications on creating a defensible space and firescaping.**

Plants That Resist Fire

Flowers

Fragaria x *ananassa* (strawberry) – Low growing; fire resistant if watered, and edible too. Fort Laramie, an everbearing variety, is hardy throughout the region. Not tolerant of alkaline or clayey soils. Insect pollinated and low allergy. Blooms June to August, depending on variety; Zones 2–8, depending on variety.

Helianthemum (rockrose or sun rose) – Low-growing, silvery leaved evergreen perennials with one-inch flowers in summer in colors from red to orange, yellow, rose, and white. Moderate water needs, such as well-drained soil. At high elevations, mulch with evergreen branches in winter. Insect pollinated and low allergy. Zones 4–9.

Sedum lanceolatum (yellow stonecrop) – Native succulent wildflower with a basal rosette of tiny leaves that turn reddish in fall, stalk of golden yellow flowers in spring to early summer. Spreads naturally; water stored in succulent leaves resists fire. Insect pollinated and low allergy. Zones 3–6.

Grasses

Low-growing native grass mixes that, if kept green and mowed,
   form low-water-use lawns that serve as defensible space
   (see "Gardening Resources" for native seed sources). A
   mix of equal parts of blue grama, Arizona fescue, stream-
   bank wheatgrass, western wheatgrass, and Indian
   ricegrass will thrive at elevations from 3,500 to 7,000 feet,
   depending on exposure. Plant female cultivars for allergy
   prevention.

Shrubs

Cotoneaster horizontalis (spreading cotoneaster) – Easy-care
   nonnative shrub with small leaves and berries that attract
   birds. Relatively drought tolerant and low growing, but
   hardy only to around 8,000 feet. Insect pollinated and low
   allergy.

Trees

Betula glandulosa (bog birch) – Tall (to eight feet) riparian shrub
   with rounded, toothed leaves that turn red or orange in
   autumn. Fire resistant only if well watered. Wind pollinated.
   Zones 3–6.

Populus angustifolia (narrowleaf cottonwood) – Native mountain riparian tree with shiny deciduous leaves that turn
   amber in autumn. Forms clumps from root-sprouts and
   requires regular irrigation. Plant female cultivars; avoid
   cottonless or male trees. Zones 3–5.

INVADERS

WEEDS
What's a Weed?

*Weed—any plant or vegetation ...
interfering with the objectives or
requirements of people.*
—European Weed Research Society Statutes, article III, 1975

The definition of a weed depends on the context. One person's weed may be another's wildflower. A weed to a rancher may be valuable wildlife habitat to a biologist. A weed is simply an unwanted plant. A rose could be a weed in an onion patch. The most harmful weeds are nonnative species that endanger the health of native ecosystems.

Managing weeds involves knowing the unwanted plant's life strategy, its reproductive choices; specifically, is it an annual, biennial, or a perennial plant? Annuals are ephemeral: they sprout, bloom, and die all in a brief period while conditions are hospitable. Biennials usually sprout a leaf rosette and spend their first year making food, then bloom and set seed the following year. Perennials are tougher because they are adapted to survive more than one season, so they are more difficult to eradicate.

Eliminating annual weeds means eliminating the seeds, since the plants die soon after reproducing. With perennials, eliminating the root system is critical, since it may sprout new plants. String trimmers and mowers don't eliminate weeds. In fact they spread annual seeds around, ensuring a second crop. Perennials can sprout from the base left by the trimmer. Biennials can't root-sprout, so they're more like two-year annuals than perennials.

The surest way to get rid of annuals is with good old-fashioned hand labor—pull them up. Dispose of them carefully by bagging them or burning them (check local ordinances on burning). Don't compost weeds with seeds as compost pile temperatures aren't high enough to kill the seeds.

Killing or digging up the roots is the only way to eliminate perennial weeds. The best strategy varies with the particular species and can be as simple as employing a dandelion digger or as difficult as the repeated spraying needed to outwit noxious weeds. (See "Outsmarting the Invaders," page 77 and "Noxious Weeds," page 79.)

Green Today and Gone Tomorrow

Annuals are the plants that pop up suddenly after snowmelt, rains, or the first good soak you give your garden, then vanish just as quickly when conditions change. They are the marigolds, cosmos, petunias, California poppies, lettuce, dill, herbs, and vegetables we love. They also include the prostrate amaranth, cheatgrass, pigweed, tumbleweed, spiny sow thistle, kochia, and annual bluegrass we curse.

Annuals live by a party-till-you-drop strategy. They take advantage of changing conditions. When moisture is abundant, they sprout, grow, and bloom copiously. As soon as drying soil or plunging temperatures signal that the party is over, these plants go into a frenzy of reproduction, producing copious amounts of seeds, and then wither and die.

Persistent weeding can essentially eliminate annuals, but you must pull and dispose of the plants before they drop seeds. Removing successive generations will eventually exhaust the local seed source, but some annual seeds can persist in the soil for decades.

Tip **To control large areas of annual weeds, rototill or disk the weeds into the soil before they set seed or you'll just multiply the problem. Or, smother them before they set seed by covering the soil with cardboard, a thick layer of newspaper, or black plastic. Anchor it with stones or bricks and leave in place for an entire growing season.**

One of the best ways to control annual weeds before planting new lawns, perennial beds, or vegetable gardens is to water and fertilize then wait a week or two for weed seeds to sprout. Pull the weeds, disturbing the soil as little as possible, and then plant.

Outsmarting the Invaders: The Region's Top Garden Weeds and How to Defeat Them

Convolvulus arvensis (bindweed) – A perennial, vining, morning glory relative with small white flowers and heart-shaped leaves. Dig up the deep taproot or pull the stems every few weeks during the growing season (this eventually exhausts the root). As a last resort, treat with glyphosate when bindweed is actively growing but before it has set seed.

Cirsium canadense (Canada thistle) – This colony-forming thistle begins as a basal rosette of wavy spined leaves and eventually sprouts stems topped with clusters of small pink-purple flower heads that produce abundant, wind-borne seeds. This aggressive weed is native to southeastern Eurasia. Spray plants with undiluted white household vinegar, then cut and dispose of flower heads. Older plants may require multiple treatments.

Bromus tectorum (cheatgrass or downy brome) – A Mediterranean native with nodding seeds bearing a fingertip-length, needlelike appendage protruding from each seed. Cheatgrass sprouts in winter and spring, greening whole areas of landscape, and then dries out. Hence the name cheat, since it initially looks like good forage. It is extremely flammable and thus a serious threat to native ecosystems. Control by hand pulling or disking before it sets seed.

Malva neglecta (cheeseweed) – A low, spreading mallow with small pinkish white flowers; rounded, lobed leaves; and hard, disk-shaped seedpods. Depending on the zone, it may be an annual, biennial, or short-lived perennial. Pull young plants; dig older plants with a dandelion digger to get the large taproot.

Poa annua (annual bluegrass) – A winter annual in lawns, flower beds, and vegetable gardens. This short, soft grass with whitish seed heads forms tufts that are easily pulled by hand. In lawns, use corn gluten meal in spring, which thickens the existing turf to crowd out weeds.

Taraxacum officinale (dandelion) – The common name comes from the deeply toothed leaves. Dandelion is a corruption of the French *dente de lion*, or "lion's tooth." Dandelions are an important nectar source for early-emerging butterflies and other pollinators, so a few are beneficial. To control large infestations, hand dig with a dandelion digger to get the large taproot and apply corn gluten meal in spring to thicken the lawn turf and crowd out seedlings.

Salsola siberica (tumbleweed or Russian thistle) – A native of
  arid Eurasia that arrived in North America with flaxseed in
  the late 1800s. Sprouts are bright green with long, needlelike leaves and a red-striped stem. They quickly grow into
  ball-shaped plants up to six feet across. When the plant
  dries, a special layer at the base of the stem breaks, free-
  ing the tumbleweed to roll with the wind, dropping seeds
  with every bounce. Hand weed when young or rototill large
  areas before the plants set seed.

Ulmus pumila (Chinese elm) – A weedy tree native to Eurasia,
  once planted for windbreaks and shade. Grows up to thirty
  feet tall, usually with a single trunk. Its strongly serrated
  leaves are shiny green but develop a lacy appearance
  midsummer from elm leaf beetle grazing. The abundant
  seedlings are a nuisance. Pull young seedlings; cut older
  trees to the base and spray sprouts with glyphosate.

Tip **Never use synthetic herbicides around food
  plants, especially vegetable, herb, or edible flower gardens. Always follow the label directions. Using the wrong
  herbicide can be disastrous to desirable plants. More herbicide is not better. Never use herbicides where they will
  wash into streams, lakes, ponds, or springs.**

Noxious Weeds

Some nonnative plants are so aggressive and harmful
to native ecosystems that they are labeled noxious weeds.
It is illegal to sell or plant noxious weeds in most areas.
Noxious weeds are one of the region's most pervasive
environmental problems. They dominate millions of acres of
wildlands, choking out native plants and destroying habitat
for wildlife and domestic livestock. The region's noxious
weeds include Dalmatian and yellow toadflax; diffuse,

Russian, and spotted knapweeds; leafy spurge; Russian olive; tamarisk or salt cedar; and yellow star thistle.

Gardeners sometimes still plant toadflax (also called butter and eggs), Russian olive, and tamarisk. Toadflax spreads and outcompetes native vegetation; its roots contain substances that poison grazers. Russian olive, widely planted as a windbreak and for wildlife, crowds out native species along rivers and streams. Tamarisk, a prodigiously thirsty plant, has lowered water levels and made soils salty on some 5 million acres alongside the West's rivers, streams, and lakes.

Tip **You can help prevent the spread of noxious weeds by learning to identify them and eradicating them where you find them. Ask your County Extension agent or provincial government for information on toxic weeds in your area.**

When Good Plants Go Bad

Imagine a perennial plant that thrives with little care, rewarding you with cheerful blossoms every year. Then one year it suddenly gets out of control, popping up in your lawn and vegetable garden, your neighbor's yard, and even the nearby park.

That's a typical scenario for invasive weeds, according to researchers. Roughly half of the estimated three hundred invasive weed species in the United States were introduced as ornamentals. Plants brought here from other places may behave well for years or even decades before some environmental or physiological change causes them to go wild.

Our generally arid climate controls some species—until an unusually wet period allows them to multiply, and then suddenly they are out of control. That's how toadflax and oxeye daisy hopped from gardens to wildlands where they crowd out native wildflowers.

Other species remain mild mannered until they hybridize with a species from which they once were isolated. Mixing genes allows the resultant hybrids some competitive advantage, such as better resistance to grazing insects. Researchers say that is what has allowed tamarisk to swiftly take over riparian areas in the arid West.

Still other species simply outcompete the natives by either poisoning them or smothering them. Plants manufacture a wide range of herbicides and pesticides to defeat competing species and repel grazing insects.

So be careful what you plant!

Tip **The Nature Conservancy lists problem garden plants on their Web site, along with helpful identification photographs (http://nature.org/initiatives/invasivespecies/features/).**

The Law of Empty Spaces

Bare ground doesn't stay bare for long. Seeds germinate, roots sprout in the soil, and pretty soon the formerly empty space is filled with growth. That's good if the plants are those you want; it's bad if they're unwanted invaders.

Ecologically speaking, bare ground is an unfilled niche, a habitat that is not occupied. Unoccupied habitat doesn't remain that way for long, because there are plenty of plants ready to colonize it. Thus the best way to minimize weed problems is to minimize bare ground.

In perennial beds, xeriscaped areas, or patches of wild plantings, use rock or other mulches to keep bare soil covered. In vegetable gardens, reduce the need for hoeing and tilling by using weed cloth or other porous ground covers and in winter, plant cover crops as living mulch. (See "To Mulch or Not to Mulch," page 46, for more information.)

Thicken lawns with amendments and natural weed-controlling agents such as corn gluten meal; dense turf leaves no unfilled niches where weeds can sprout. Use ground cover plants between paving stones and along the edges of walks, patios, and flower beds.

Shade also defeats most weeds, because they are adapted to germinate in the bare soil and bright light of disturbed ground. Evergreen trees and shrubs cast shade year-round, greatly reducing weed germination. But shade may also discourage desirable species, so plan carefully for shade plantings. (See "Life in the Dark," page 29.)

A Rose by Any Other Name: Decoding Scientific Names

With their multiple syllables and unrecognizable words, scientific names seem incomprehensible. But scientific (botanical) names often tell you something about the plant or its discovery.

Learning scientific names helps you avoid confusion when there are multiple common names for the same plant and common names shared by many very different plants. (A sage can be a pungent six-foot-tall wild shrub in the genus *Seriphidium* of the sunflower family, a culinary herb or an ornamental annual in the genus *Salvia* of the mint family, or one of many horticultural varieties of Southwestern native shrubs with red to purple flowers much in demand for xeriscaping, also in the genus *Salvia* of the mint family.)

It's not so difficult to decode scientific names with a dictionary that includes Greek and Roman suffixes and prefixes. The first part of the binomial (two part) name is the genus. It is always capitalized and usually is a classical name referring to a group of closely related plants in the same botanical family. The second part is the specific epithet designating the particular species, or distinct kind of plant. It isn't capitalized unless it is from a proper noun and it is usually a descriptive term. For example, *Malus domestica*: *Malus* means apple in Latin, domestica is easy to translate as "domestic."

A species is a genetically distinct plant that doesn't breed with other similar plants in the wild. A subspecies is a genetically identical population of a species with distinct characteristics. A form is usually a geographically defined population. A variety is a horticultural type, while a cultivar is a cultivated variety of one particular plant, often created through hybridizing.

Take the daffodil. In the language of science, daffodils, narcissus, and jonquils all belong to the genus *Narcissus*, named for the youth in Greek mythology who fell in love with his own reflection. In common terms, most people interchange the names, but *jonquil* refers to the narrow-leaved species with swept-back petals and its cultivars, *Narcissus jonquilla*. The original species, from which all daffodils were bred, include *N. bulbocodium* ("bulblike head") and *N. cyclamineus* ("cyclamenlike").

Designing a Low-Allergy Garden

Gardening is a healthy activity, combining physical exercise with the emotional and spiritual benefits of connecting with nature. Gardening also makes growing numbers of us sick with wheezing, running noses, itching eyes, and sore throats. What's going on?

Horticulturist Thomas Leo Ogren identifies the problem as an unnatural sexual imbalance in our cultivated landscapes. He points out that by planting fruitless varieties—male plants instead of messy female ones—we've clogged the air and our lungs with pollen, which comes from the male plants.

Some plants are inherently allergenic. The oils on poison ivy, for instance, cause skin rashes. The strong fragrances of plants such as freesias can irritate nasal passages. Wind-dispersed pollen of plants such as ragweed causes hay fever in an increasing number of people.

But Ogren and a growing number of other allergy researchers assert that we've caused a surge in the frequency of respiratory allergies—from 2 to 5 percent of Americans in the late 1950s to 38 percent in 1999—by surrounding ourselves with male plants. Ogren contends that pollen has gone from a mere irritant to a serious biopollutant.

The overproliferation of pollen stems from our ignorance about plant sex. Plants use pollen for sexual reproduction. Flowers are fertilized when pollen from one plant lands on the pistil, the female sex organ, of another plant of the same species. Some plants' flowers contain both male and female sexual organs; others flowers are only male or only female. Separate-sex flowers may occur on the same plant (as with corn) or on separate plants (as with cottonwood trees).

In order to move pollen from plant to plant, some species produce fancy flowers in bright colors with nectar to lure visits from mobile creatures such as insects, birds, and bats. Others throw literally tons of feather-light pollen to the wind. The latter are the problem plants. By planting millions of them, we have increased the airborne pollen concentration beyond what our lungs can handle.

▲ ▽ ▲ ▲ ▽ ▲ ▽ ▲ ▽ ▲ ▽ ▲ ▽ ▲ ▽

MAKING YOUR GARDEN A HEALTHIER PLACE
Remove and replace male-only plants, especially large
shrubs and trees, because they produce the largest volume of pollen. The first priority is to get rid of male-only
plants located close to windows and doors and around
gathering places such as swimming pools and patios.
Plant female-only plants. Their sticky pistils will trap
excess pollen from the air and their fruits will attract birds
and butterflies to your garden. For holly and some other
dioecious plants (male on one plant, female on another),
you need both male and female if you want the ornamental berries. Check your lawn grass: if it's a male-only
cultivar (bluegrass pollen is particularly allergenic), this
may be a good time to replace it.

▲ ▽ ▲ ▲ ▽ ▲ ▽ ▲ ▽ ▲ ▽ ▲ ▽ ▲ ▽

Plants That Won't Get Out of Control

**Plants native to your ecosystem are the best choices. If those
don't suit, here are some suggestions.**

Flowers
Antirrhinum majus (snapdragon) – This familiar annual garden
plant with its spikes of two-lipped flowers in many colors is
not native. Unlike its tougher cousin, toadflax, or butter-
and-eggs, it stays in the garden. Insect pollinated and low
allergy. Blooms all summer with deadheading. Annual.
Coreopsis verticillata 'Zagreb' (narrow-leaved coreopsis) – A
compact cultivar of 'Moonbeam' coreopsis with star-shaped
yellow flowers and narrow leaves. Long blooming, deer
resistant, and hardy to Zone 3. Insect pollinated and low
allergy. Blooms July through frost.

Geranium 'Johnson's Blue' (blue cranesbill) – A long-blooming cultivar of Himalayan cranesbill with two-inch-wide blue flowers. Not drought tolerant, but thrives with little additional water. Hardy to Zone 2. Caution: it could spread if watered too frequently. Insect pollinated and low allergy. Blooms June through frost.

Paeonia lactiflora (garden peony) – Long-lived plants that produce fragrant, beautiful single or double flowers above dark green foliage in early summer. Requires enriched soil, regular watering, and fertilizing after blooming and again in fall. Hardy to Zone 2, low allergy.

Shrubs

Perovskia atriplicifolia (Russian sage) – A long-blooming, drought-tolerant native of Eurasia with lacy foliage and tall stalks bearing spikes of tiny, slate blue flowers. Hardy to Zone 4 or below if in a warm microclimate. Insect pollinated and low allergy. Blooms all summer.

Trees

Acer saccharinum 'Northline' (northline silver maple) – A beautiful, fast-growing deciduous tree with silvery undersides on deeply notched leaves. Hardy to Zone 2. Adapted to many soil types; not drought hardy. Great for shade, but shallow roots will heave pavement and foundations. A female cultivar pulls pollen from the air.

PESTS LARGE and SMALL
Who's Eating My Garden?

*Environmentalism is not just about
"purple mountain majesties"
and saving places;
it's about understanding that our lives
depend on the natural environment.*

—Chef Alice Waters, in an interview in
Nature Conservancy, Summer 2003

"Plant it and they will come!" rings true when hordes of pests descend like locusts on our plants. Because garden plants are succulent and nutritious compared to wild plants, they attract consumers of all sorts: leaf gobblers, hole cutters, stem girdlers, sap sippers, tip killers, borers, browsers, and parasites.

These invaders simply seek what we all desire: food, shelter, and the chance to reproduce. Understanding their needs and life histories—the niche they occupy—can help you get them under control if they're harmful or tolerate them if they're not.

Nibblers go for leaves and tender sprouts. Grasshoppers, leaf miners, caterpillars, slugs, and rabbits munch whole leaves. Leaf-cutter bees nibble at the edges, cutting neat circles to plug their brood chambers. Army cutworms topple the plant for its leaves.

Sap sippers, such as scale, aphids, and thrips, attach themselves to leaf undersides, shoots, or trunks to feed on the sugary fluid in the plant's vascular tissue.

Browsers go for woodier material. Deer and elk nip off tender branch tips and nibble anything sweet—they love tulips. Porcupines prefer bark for the sugary sap underneath. Squirrels, grouse, and spruce budworms favor nutritious tree buds.

Borers munch their way through wood. Some, such as carpenter bees and carpenter ants, specialize in eating deadwood. Others, including pinebark beetles, bore through live tree trunks.

Root munchers hang out underground, feeding on live or decaying material. Pocket gophers favor bulbs; scarab beetle larvae munch grass roots; cicada larvae suck root sap.

Internal pests include rusts and mildews, and fungi that thread through the plant's vascular system, appearing on the surface only to cast their spores to the wind. Bacteria and viruses are microscopic parasites that live in and around plant cells.

Tip **The best way to control garden pest problems is by growing healthy plants. Thriving plants resist pests and recover most quickly. Synthetic pesticides should be a last resort because they are dangerous. Pesticides are implicated in human health issues, cause environmental problems, and kill beneficial insect populations in addition to the pests.**

Outwitting the Invaders: A Primer on the Region's Top Animal, Insect, and Fungus Pests

Aphids – Curling and distorted new growth often signal aphids. Aphids weaken but don't usually kill plants. The viruses they carry, such as cucumber mosaic virus, are the real problem. Avoid overwatering and remove annual weeds as they are alternate hosts for some species of aphids. Provide a habitat for beneficial insects (the good bugs that get the bad guys) such as ladybird beetles, lacewings, and parasitic wasps. They promote long-term control. For spot control, spray plants with two tablespoons of liquid dish soap dissolved in a gallon of warm water. Add a couple of drops of vegetable oil to the solution to make it stick better to the leaves. Spray the tops and bottoms of leaves every seven to ten days.

Army cutworms – Control these miller moth larvae by keeping your garden free of weeds, especially in late summer when the moths lay eggs. Ground beetles, rove beetles, spiders, toads, and garter snakes all devour cutworms.

Cucumber and potato beetles – These are small beetles with conspicuous striped wing covers that feed on vegetable and fruit crops. Striped cucumber beetles devour the leaves of plants in the cucumber family including melons, squash, and cucumbers. Colorado potato beetles munch on the leaves of potatoes and others in the potato family, including eggplant, tomatoes, peppers, and ground cherries. The most effective control is to pick the beetles off plants and drop them into a bucket of soapy water. Lady beetle larvae prey on the larvae of potato beetles.

Deer – Macrobrowsers such as deer, elk, and even moose can take a macrobite out of gardens. Landscaping with plants they don't relish is most effective. (See "Indigestible Plants," page 97.) Fencing is the next best bet—your fence must be at least eight feet high for deer. If you cage individual plants, remember that deer on their hind legs can reach more than six feet high. Additionally, deep snow extends the reach of all browsers. Spreading a fragrant deterrent, from stinky soap to Zoodoo™ (lion and other zoo animals' dung) may work, but success varies. Repellent sprays are effective but expensive and must be reapplied frequently.

Grasshoppers (and Mormon crickets) – En masse, grasshoppers and Mormon crickets can shred a garden, munching plants down to bare stubs. The most effective control is handpicking. Baits containing a microbial grasshopper parasite work slowly and only kill nymphs—the young grasshoppers. Providing habitat for grasshopper-eating birds, such as house wrens and American kestrels, may be a good preventive technique. Chickens also relish grasshoppers. Floating row covers protect vegetable gardens and fruit crops.

Leaf-cutter bees – If it looks like someone has attacked the edges of your shrub and tree leaves with a hole punch, you've got leaf-cutter bees. That's a good thing, because these bees are important pollinators of many plants. Their nibbling doesn't harm the plants. Female bees use the cutouts to plug egg chambers in their nest holes.

Pinebark beetles and Ips beetles – Numerous small holes exuding drippy sap on the trunks and limbs of pines, Douglas firs, spruces, and true firs point to an infestation of these native beetles. Females bore into the tree's bark to lay their eggs and the larvae feed on the wood as they grow. Healthy trees expel the beetle larvae with their sap pressure, but trees stressed by drought, heat, and crowding cannot. Keeping trees watered and thinned is the best defense.

Once a tree is infested, even pesticides won't save it. Cut down infested trees and chip, burn, debark, and dispose of the wood to prevent the beetles from spreading. Do not use wood chips from infested trees.

Powdery mildew – The whitish powder is the spores of this group of fungi that feed on dead or dying plant tissue. Spray the affected plant with a jet of water to wash off and kill the spores, then pick and dispose of infected leaves and shoots. A mixture of one gallon of water with two tablespoons of baking soda, several drops of Ivory Liquid soap, and several drops of vegetable oil sprayed weekly on the tops and bottoms of the plant's leaves works well, without the possibility of spreading the spores. Do not spray if it is above 80° F. Powdery mildew may be a sign of a distressed plant; healthy plants are most resistant.

Scale – These sap-sipping aphid relatives look like tiny, hard bumps on the trunks and branches of deciduous trees. They armor themselves against predators and insecticides with a shell-like scale. Gentle rubbing with a nylon kitchen dish scrubber removes scale.

Scarab beetles – Brown spots in lawn turf either result from root-grazing scarab beetle larvae or nitrogen burn from dog urine. Probe a dead spot with a trowel. Whitish, comma-shaped grubs in the soil may be scarab beetle larvae or larvae of Japanese beetles or June bugs. Regular soil aeration prevents grub or larvae damage. Treatment with applications of powdered milky spore disease (a naturally occurring bacterium called *Bacillus thuringiensis* or Bt) at the proper time of year will control the grubs for ten years or more providing that you do not use any pesticide on the lawn, as it will kill the milky spore.

Slugs – Slugs use rasplike teeth on their undersides to devour the plants they slime across. A dry and uncrowded garden makes for poor slug habitat. If slugs are a problem, avoid mulches such as grass clippings and clear out dead material around plants. Borders of wood ash and diatomaceous earth repel slugs but must be reapplied frequently—especially after rain or watering. Copper strips are longer lasting. Copper repels by creating an electrical charge with the slime.

Spider mites – These minute arachnids (spider relatives) sip sap from shrubs and trees, particularly those stressed by drought or covered with a thick layer of dust. Yellow-speckled or bronzy leaves reveal the presence of spider mites, as do moving flecks of red, yellow, or green—the actual mites. Wash spider mites off with a strong stream of water. Lacewing larvae and other insect predators eat spider mites.

Tobacco or tomato hornworms – Caterpillars are picky eaters, munching one species or a group of related species. Tomato hornworms, named for the prominent horn at their rear end, feed on tomatoes and other plants in the same family including peppers, eggplants, tomatillos, and potatoes. These odd-looking caterpillars metamorphose into the beautiful hovering hawk moths that pollinate night-blooming garden flowers such as evening primroses and four-o'clocks. If you cannot tolerate them, handpick the caterpillars and drop them into a bucket of soapy water or use a *Bacillus thuringiensis* spray.

▲ ▼ ▲ ▲ ▼ ▲ ▼ ▲ ▼ ▲ ▼ ▲ ▼ ▲ ▼

WORM VERSUS CATERPILLAR AND GRUB In common usage, any insect larva with an elongated body, from a tomato hornworm to an earthworm is called a worm. The word is derived from the Old Norse term *verm*, for serpent. In biology, however, a tomato hornworm is more correctly a caterpillar, and an earthworm is the true worm. *Worm* is reserved for the slender, very elongated bodies of those invertebrates that live in water or burrow in the soil, from roundworms to earthworms.

▲ ▼ ▲ ▲ ▼ ▲ ▼ ▲ ▼ ▲ ▼ ▲ ▼ ▲ ▼

Garden Sex: Pollinator–Plant Relationships

Flowers are all about sex. If plants depended on vegetative reproduction—cloning themselves—there would be no reason for flowers. The flowers of wind-pollinated plants are tiny and inconspicuous. Those of plants that use pollinators explode with the colors, scents, and forms that make them so beloved of gardeners.

Plants that depend on flower-hopping pollinators spend a tremendous amount of energy attracting them. They manufacture special pigments that make their flowers as visible as neon signs. They make nectar, a nutritious sugary liquid, and secrete it deep inside the flower. They grow petals in intricate shapes, decorated with guide-stripes and dotted lines that lead pollinators to the inner bounty.

The usual arrangement is to trade food for sex. To reach the food, the pollinator must brush past the sticky surface of the stigma, fertilizing the flower with pollen collected from another plant's blossoms. Flower architecture in these species aims to entice the winged, crawling, or hopping pollinators as well as prevent self fertilization.

A dizzying array of creatures act as pollinators: ants, bees of all kinds, flower flies, wasps, beetles, butterflies, moths, hummingbirds, warblers, doves, bats, mice, and humans. Some pollinators are specific to one species; others are generalists. A healthy garden welcomes pollinators of all kinds.

▲ ▼ ▲ ▲ ▼ ▲ ▼ ▲ ▼ ▲ ▼ ▲ ▼ ▲ ▼

NIGHT GARDENS Flowers that open in the evening and close during the day, such as evening primroses, datura, moonflowers, and four-o'clocks, employ moon-bright blossoms and sensuous fragrances to lure nocturnal pollinators. A night garden planted near a patio or deck gives glimpses of this dusk magic. Watching the tightly spiraled bud of an evening primrose unfurl to welcome the touch of a hovering hawk moth is unforgettable, as is the sight and sound of the hawk moth—so similar to a hummingbird.

▲ ▼ ▲ ▲ ▼ ▲ ▼ ▲ ▼ ▲ ▼ ▲ ▼ ▲ ▼

The Killing Fields: The Perils of Pesticides

When synthetic pesticides were introduced in the 1950s, their promise was to rid the world of legions of harmful invaders, from dandelions to potato beetles. Since then, Americans have spent billions upon billions of dollars on these chemicals, while their targets have become increasingly resistant and the pesticides themselves have often backfired.

Pesticide use has been implicated in large-scale groundwater contamination, poisoning of aquatic ecosystems, disastrous reproductive abnormalities in fish and other aquatic creatures, and increased rates of human cancers.

Although most research on the detrimental effects of pesticide use has been based upon agricultural use, home gardens may be even more dangerous. Home gardeners apply the equivalent of ten to fifteen times the amount of pesticide per acre that farmers use.

The best way to minimize pest problems in your garden is to maintain healthy plants. If a plant begins to look diseased or shows signs of being munched, check it carefully. Is it water stressed? Does it need soil amendments? Is it getting too much sun or shade? Research shows that healthy plants can repel normal levels of pests, from grasshoppers to bark beetles.

Plants invented pesticides: they produce an astonishing variety of compounds that act as herbicides and insecticides, some of which are now used as alternatives to more harmful synthetic pesticides. In fact, plants with their own naturally occurring pesticides are the basis of the practice of companion planting, where pesticide-producing plants, such as marigolds, are interplanted with edible plants, such as basil or tomatoes.

If you must use pesticides, follow the label directions carefully, using as much caution with the plants as with yourself. Pesticides kill. And not just their weed and pest targets: they can also kill beneficial species, including you.

▲ ▼ ▲ ▲ ▼ ▲ ▼ ▲ ▼ ▲ ▼ ▲ ▼ ▲ ▼

BATS – NATURAL PEST CONTROL A single Myotis or mouse-eared bat can consume up to 500 insects an hour, including mosquitoes. Contrary to popular myth, bats are not blind—they can see, but they depend on sophisticated echolocation systems to navigate in total darkness. So precise is their ability to "hear" the surrounding terrain in the dark that they can detect and avoid objects as fine as a human hair. Bats also have a lower incidence of rabies than many other wild animals, disproving another myth about these fascinating flying mammals. Bat Conservation International's Web site, www.batcon.org/ has plans for bat boxes and other information about making bats welcome.

▲ ▼ ▲ ▲ ▼ ▲ ▼ ▲ ▼ ▲ ▼ ▲ ▼ ▲ ▼

Who Eats Whom?

How can you invite wildlife into your yard while still maintaining your prized flowers, vegetables, fruits, and herbs? Learning who is who and who eats whom is important to enjoying wildlife in your garden.

Start by paying attention to what happens in your garden. Use field guides and garden books to identify birds, animals, insects, and other garden visitors. Take notes: Who is the visitor? When do you see it? What is it doing? Where does it hang out? Like a field biologist learning the inhabitants of an alpine meadow, you are learning the inhabitants of your garden ecosystem.

Hummingbirds are easy wildlife to welcome. These jeweled flyers are not only beautiful and fascinating to watch, they are also master pollinators of certain kinds of plants. In addition, nesting hummingbirds help control garden pests by feeding their nestlings small insects, including aphids and spiders. Plant red, orange, or dark pink tube-shaped, nectar-bearing flowers to attract hummingbirds. A patch of scarlet buglar penstemons, for example, will not only reward you with vivid flower spikes in spring, it will also attract hummingbirds from miles around. Indian paintbrush (any *Castilleja* species) is another hummingbird favorite, as are hummingbird mint (any *Agastache* species) and red bee balm (*Monarda didyma*).

Tip **In our arid region, water draws wildlife. Set out a shallow pan of water filled with gravel in a sunny spot to attract butterflies, from tiny shimmering blues to huge tiger swallowtails.**

▲ ▼ ▲ ▲ ▼ ▲ ▼ ▲ ▼ ▲ ▼ ▲ ▼ ▲ ▼

RESTORING HABITAT The news is full of horror stories about human activities destroying habitat for species large and small, common and rare. Often we feel helpless and overwhelmed by the magnitude of the problem. One way to give something back is by "re-wilding" a place in your neighborhood: a piece of your yard, a park, an urban creek, or a degraded wetland. Start small: learn what native grasses and wildflowers grow in your neighborhood and plant a wild corner in your yard. As the natives grow, watch who arrives to take up residence. The Web site www.nwf.org/backyardwildlifehabitat/ is a good place to go for ideas (see the "wildlife gallery"), as is www.audubon.org/bird/at_home/index.html (see especially "rethink your lawn"), as well as www.xerces.org/poll/index.htm (see "backyard pollinator habitat"), or a local nature center.

▲ ▼ ▲ ▲ ▼ ▲ ▼ ▲ ▼ ▲ ▼ ▲ ▼ ▲ ▼

Indigestible Plants

Look at other plant lists for more indigestible species.

Flowers

Allium christophii (star of Persia) – A wild onion, native to the
mountains of Iraq and Iran, with spectacular ten-inch-
diameter flower heads in lavender-pink in midsummer.
Grows to two feet tall. Not drought tolerant, but long
persistent and easy care if watered regularly. Attracts
butterflies, low allergy. Zones 4–7.

Delphinium elatum 'Blue Fountains' (Blue Fountains delphinium)–
A shorter version of the familiar Pacific Giants delphinium
that doesn't require staking, so it is more suitable to the
arid and windy climates of much of the region. Flower
stalks to thirty inches tall. Requires enriched soils and
regular watering. Insect pollinated and low allergy.
Blooms June through July; Zones 3–10.

Eriogonum umbellatum (sulfur buckwheat) – Native wildflower
with showy sulfur yellow flower clusters in spring and
rounded evergreen leaves that turn plum colored in winter.
Low water use; requires well-drained soil; hardy to Zone 4.
Attracts butterflies, low allergy.

Rheum x *cultorum* (rhubarb) – A perennial with large, crinkled
leaves held high on thick, red-tinted stalks; some varieties
have grass green stalks. Dramatic as a landscape plant,
especially in flower in summer. Leaves are poisonous; stalks
used in pies, sweet sauces, and jams. Requires regular
water; hardy to Zone 2. Insect pollinated and low allergy.

Tagetes erecta (African marigold) – Aromatic annuals. Easy to
grow from seed. Varieties range from single- to double-
flowered in shades of pastel and bright yellows, oranges,
and maroons. Plants range from six inches to six feet tall.
Tall varieties need more water and require staking. Aroma
discourages grazers; pollen may be allergenic. Annual.

Shrubs

Spirea plenifolia 'Plena' (bridalwreath spirea) — Tough perennial
shrub from eastern Asia with arching branches to six feet
tall that are lined with small, double white flowers from
spring through midsummer. Small dark green leaves turn
yellow to red in fall. Can survive drought periods, but does
best with some regular water. Thrives in all soils except
saline. Insect pollinated and low allergy. Zones 3–8.

Plants That Attract Wildlife

Flowers

Aquilegia caerulea (Colorado blue columbine) — A spring- and
early summer–blooming native to the Rockies with blue-
and-white, long-spurred flowers that attract hummingbirds
and butterflies. Tolerates light shade, requires well-drained
soils. Insect pollinated and low allergy. Zones 3–6.

Asclepias tuberosa (butterfly weed) — An eastern North American milkweed species with slender leaves and terminal
clusters of brilliant orange flowers in mid- to late summer.
Cultivated varieties may be red, yellow, orange, or
bicolored. Inflated pods and silky seeds follow the flowers.
Needs moderate water; attracts butterflies; low allergy.
Zones 4–9.

Echinacea purpurea 'Magnus' (Magnus purple coneflower) —
A cultivar of the native from eastern and central North
America with large purple flowers atop two- to four-foot
stalks for great late summer color. Needs moderate water;
attracts butterflies. Zones 4–9.

Lupinus hybrids (lupine) – Perennial hybrids from native western North American species in the pea family. New Generation hybrids are sturdier and longer lived than the old-fashioned Russell hybrids and come in more colors, from yellow and pink to red, blue, and purple. Needs moderate water; adds nitrogen to the soil through nitrogen- fixing bacteria that live in its root nodules. Attracts hummingbirds and butterflies; low allergy. Blooms June to mid-July; Zones 3–8.

Oenothera macrocarpa (evening primrose) – Native to the Great Plains with huge, night-blooming, yellow flowers; A spectacular addition to the evening garden, attracting sphinx moths and hawk moths. Drought tolerant once established; low allergy. Blooms June through August; Zones 4–8.

Phlox paniculata 'David' (David garden phlox) – Not drought tolerant, but a beautiful addition to well-watered gardens. Snowy white flowers on tall plants in June; mildew-resistant foliage. Attracts butterflies; low allergy. Zones 4–8.

Phaseolus coccineus (scarlet runner bean) – A twining, edible ornamental vine native to the New World that is perennial in warm climates but most often grown as an annual. Showy clusters of vivid red, edible flowers in summer and bright green leaves divided into three leaflets. Pods edible when less than three inches long. Or, allow to grow to maturity and use as a dried bean. Needs regular water; attracts hummingbirds; low allergy. ones. Annual.

Acknowledgments

Thanks to my mother, Joan C. Tweit, who served as my ace researcher, and to my dad, Robert C. Tweit, who mended my occasionally fractured science.

Thanks also to the many gardeners and landscape designers who have educated and inspired me over the years, especially my brother Bill Tweit and my sister-in-law Lucy Winter, Letitia Hitz, Ann Palormo, Blanche Sobottke, and Beverly Gray. Thanks as well to the native plant providers whose knowledge and plants have enriched my yard and neighborhood: Lorri and Gary at Pleasant Avenue Nursery, Buena Vista, Colorado, and Alex and Suzanne at Western Native Seed, Coaldale, Colorado.

This book would not have come to life without the urging of Marlene Blessing, former editor-in-chief of Fulcrum Publishing, who convinced me that I had something to say to other gardeners. I owe big thanks to the current staff of Fulcrum, including Sam Scinta for his encouragement; stellar editors Faith Marcovecchio and Katie Raymond, who made my words shine; Dianne Howie, who asked me years ago if I would write something for Fulcrum—this is for you, Dianne!; and designer and illustrator extraordinaire Ann W. Douden, with whom I've been privileged to work on two previous books. Thanks also to Mindy Dwyer for the cover illustration, and to the staff in publicity, marketing, sales, and distribution, without whom the books wouldn't reach the readers. You're the best!

And special thanks to my husband, Richard Cabe, whose artist's eye shows me how to see and who supports me in whatever I do, and my wonderful daughter, Molly Cabe, who loves plants too.

Gardening Resources

BOOKS

Bormann, F. Herbert, et. al. *Redesigning the American Lawn: A Search for Environmental Harmony,* 2nd ed. New Haven, Conn.: Yale University Press, 2001.

A highly readable history of the lawn, including environmental effects and recommendations for alternatives to lawns.

Brenzel, Kathleen Norris, ed. *Sunset Western Garden Book.* Menlo Park, Calif.: Sunset Publishing Corporation, 2001.

The western garden reference, including plant selection guides for different gardening situations, a plant encyclopedia describing almost any species, variety, or cultivar planted in the West, and a very thorough primer on gardening from annuals to wildlife. Its major drawback is the Sunset climate zone system, which has been used for many years in California, but is sketchy and too unfamiliar for the rest of the West.

Cranshaw, Whitney. *Pests of the West: Prevention and Control for Today's Garden and Small Farm*, rev. ed. Golden, Colo.: Fulcrum Publishing, 1998.

> *An invaluable guide to insects, diseases, and pests, with recommendations on alternatives to pesticides. Also includes a section on attracting birds and butterflies.*

Denver Water. *Xeriscape Plant Guide: 100 Water-Wise Plants for Gardens and Landscapes*. Golden, Colo.: Fulcrum Publishing, 1996.

> *A handy illustrated guide to native and drought-adapted species, useful throughout much of the region.*

Doxon, Lynn Ellen. *High Desert Yards and Gardens*. Albuquerque, N.M.: University of New Mexico Press, 1999.

> *Great advice for gardeners in the high desert, which includes the southern part of the region, especially the lower elevations of Utah and southern and western Colorado.*

Grissell, Eric. *Insects and Gardens: In Pursuit of a Garden Ecology*. Portland, Ore.: Timber Press, 2001.

> *A fascinating illumination of the lives and habits of arthropods common in gardens; equally useful for bug-phobes or bug-lovers.*

Keen, Richard A. *Skywatch West: The Complete Weather Guide*. Golden, Colo: Fulcrum Publishing, 2004.

> *A well-written and entertaining guide to our region's weather.*

Kingsbury, Noel. *Natural Gardening in Small Spaces*. Portland, Ore.: Timber Press, 2003.

> *A paean to the beauty of gardens designed to mimic wild spaces with beautiful photographs and an abundance of ideas for residential yards and other small spaces. Written by a British landscape designer.*

Lopez, Andrea Dawn. *When Raccoons Fall Through Your Ceiling: The Handbook for Coexisting with Wildlife*. Denton, Tex.: University of North Texas Press, 2002.

> *Useful ideas for dealing with garden wildlife.*

Morrison, Sheila. *The Magic of Montana Native Plants ... a Gardener's Guide*. Missoula, Mont.: Montana Native Plant Press.

> *Great for Montana (and perhaps Alberta) gardeners.*

Ogren, Thomas Leo. *Safe Sex in the Garden and Other Propositions for An Allergy-free World*. Berkeley, Calif.: Ten Speed Press, 2003.

> *The lowdown on pollen and respiratory allergies, with advice on how to create healthy gardens.*

Springer, Lauren. *The Undaunted Garden: Planting for Weather-Resilient Beauty*. Golden, Colo.: Fulcrum Publishing, 1994.

> *The classic book on gardening in wild western climates. Beautifully written and illustrated.*

Springer, Lauren and Rob Proctor. *Passionate Gardening: Good Advice for Challenging Climates*. Golden, Colo.: Fulcrum Publishing, 2000.

> *Two garden designers describe what they love and do best in their Rocky Mountain gardens. Packed with great advice.*

Stein, Sara. *Noah's Garden: Restoring the Ecology of Our Own Back Yards*. New York: Houghton Mifflin, 1993.

> *Written for the northeast, but inspiring to any gardener seeking to understand their home landscape.*

Steingraber, Sandra. *Living Downstream: A Scientist's Personal Investigation of Cancer and the Environment*. New York: Vintage Books, 1998.

> *A heartbreakingly thorough and literate look at pesticide use and cancer by a scientist and poet who is also a cancer survivor.*

Wann, David. *The Zen of Gardening in the High and Arid West: Tips, Tools, and Techniques*. Golden, Colo.: Fulcrum Publishing, 2003.

> *A collection of short, charming essays drawing on several decades of experience gardening in the Rockies. Includes plant lists and other resources.*

Weinstein, Gayle. *Xeriscape Handbook: A How-To Guide to Natural, Resource-Wise Gardening*. Golden, Colo.: Fulcrum Publishing, 1999.

> *The subtitle says it all. Principles of gardening that use fewer resources and work with the region's environment.*

GARDEN SOCIETY NEWSLETTERS

American Penstemon Society – 1569 South Holland Court, Lakewood, CO 80226

Colorado Native Plant Society – "Aquilegia" newsletter; chapters in several Colorado locations. P.O. Box 200, Fort Collins, CO 80522-0200; www.conps.org

Horticultural Art Society of Colorado Springs – A newsletter for garden artists; also sponsors a spring plant sale at Starsmore Discovery Center near Colorado Springs. P.O. Box 7706, Colorado Springs, CO 80933-7706; (719) 475-0250

Montana Native Plant Society – "Kelseya" newsletter is very informative for gardeners. They also offer publications specific to Montana gardeners, including a source guide for native plants of Montana and guides for plants appropriate to regional Montana gardens. P.O. Box 8783, Missoula, MT 59807-8783; www.umt.edu/mnps/

Wyoming Native Plant Society – "Castilleja" newsletter. P.O. Box 3452, Laramie, WY 82071; www.uwyo.edu/wyndd/wnps/wnps_home.htm

INTERNET SITES

www.arboretum.unl.edu – Nebraska Statewide Arboretum. A wonderful resource for prairie plants and gardens including an interactive search function for native wildflowers.

www.audubon.org/bird/at_home/index.html – The Audubon Society's "Audubon At Home" site is packed with ideas for gardeners. "Learn How to Garden for Birds and Other Wildlife" has a whole list of articles on subjects from ponds to pesticides.

www.batcon.org/ – Bat Conservation International offers a treasure trove of information about these fascinating flying mammals, including a free e-newsletter and tips on how to welcome bats and their voracious appetites for flying insects to your yard.

www.botanica.com – An association of botanical gardens and arboretums. Related sites' link includes information about landscaping with native plants.

www.botanique.com – Click on "Portal" for lists of botanical gardens, other public gardens, parks, and nature trails in the United States and Canada by state and city.

www.disabilityresources.org/HORTICULTURE.html – Great resource for articles with ideas for accessible gardens.

www.ext.colostate.edu – The state agricultural extension site for Colorado, with lots of information for gardeners.

www.extension.usu.edu/ – The state agricultural extension site for Utah, with lots of information for gardeners.

www.extn.msu.montana.edu/ – The state agricultural extension site for Montana, with lots of information for gardeners.

www.firewise.org – A Web site with information on fire-wise landscaping and creating a defensible space around dwellings. Add a slash and then the state abbreviation (for example, www.firewise.org/co) for specific state pages.

www.highcountrygardens.com – A New Mexico nursery actively involved in developing native and xeriscape plants for the Rocky Mountain region and the Southwest. Excellent online newsletter with articles on high-country gardening; site also includes descriptions and photos of hundreds of plants.

www.laspilitas.com – Basic data on hundreds of native plant species including culture and wildlife values. This California nursery carries many plants suitable for the Rocky Mountain region.

www.nargs.org – North American Rock Garden Society; includes links listing many private gardens by state and city that can be visited if arranged in advance. Also describes 11,000-plus rock and alpine garden plants with cultural information and many photos.

www.nwf.org/backyardwildlifehabitat/ – The National Wildlife Federation's backyard wildlife habitat site with loads of information for how to welcome wildlife to your yard and restore habitat for your local species. It includes a free news-letter and a program to certify your yard as wildlife habitat.

www.uidaho.edu/extension/ – The state agricultural extension site for Idaho, with lots of information for gardeners.

www.uwyo.edu/ces/ceshome.htm – The state agri-cultural extension site for Wyoming, with lots of information for gardeners.

www.westernnativeseed.com – One of the most complete selections of native grass, wildflower, shrub, and tree seeds available for the Rocky Mountain region. A wide variety of grass and wildflower mixes for different areas are available, as well as custom seed mixes tailored specifically to your site.

www.xerces.org – The Xerces Society, named for the extinct Xerces Blue butterfly, is the resource for information on wild invertebrates, the legions of critters without backbones, including butterflies, moths, bees, and other pollinators. Their Web site is beautiful and full of fascinating information; it also offers publications useful to gardeners.

GARDENS and NURSERIES: INSPIRING PLACES to VISIT

ALBERTA, CANADA

Calgary Zoo and Botanical Gardens

1300 Zoo Road NE

Calgary, AB 2TE 7V6

(403) 232-9300

www.calgaryzoo.ab.ca/botanical_gardens/intro.shtml

Ornamental, greenhouse, and habitat gardens including butterfly gardens and "Canadian Wilds," which when completed will be the largest natural habitat gardens in Canada. Master gardener program, workshops, events, and tours.

Devonian Botanic Garden

University of Alberta

Edmonton, AB, T6G 2E1

(780) 987-3054

www.discoveredmonton.com/Devonian/

Gardens include a primula garden, native peoples' garden, and wetlands. Classes, horticultural collections, and links to faculty at the University of Alberta.

ARIZONA

The Arboretum at Flagstaff

4001 S. Woody Mountain Road

Flagstaff, AZ 86001

(928) 774-1442

www.thearb.org

Although not in the Rocky Mountain region proper, this arboretum and education center applies to the southern Rockies, especially to ponderosa pine ecosystems.

COLORADO

Betty Ford Alpine Garden

539 S. Frontage Road

Vail, CO 81657

(970) 476-0103

www.bettyfordalpinegardens.org

*At 8,200 feet elevation, this garden is a wonderful
resource for high-mountain gardeners, showcasing hundreds of species native to the region. Best viewing season
is from May through September.*

Denver Botanic Gardens

1005 York Street

Denver, CO 80206

(303) 331-4000

www.botanicgardens.org

*The gardens focus on plants from around the world
adapted to the Rocky Mountain region, including
an incredible rock garden, a plains garden, and a
western cottage garden. Library, workshops, lectures,
and concerts.*

Rocky Mountain Seed Company

1325 15th Street (P.O. Box 5204)

Denver, CO 80202

(303) 623-6223

(303) 623-6254 (fax)

*This 1920s storefront, with its signature gnarled gerani-
ums in pots, shelters what may be the region's oldest
family-owned seed company still in operation. It is the
place to go for information on the best horticultural
varieties to grow in the region. (Seed catalog available.)*

IDAHO

The Idaho Botanical Garden
2355 N. Penitentiary Road
Boise, ID 83712
(208) 343-8649
www.idahobotanicalgarden.org

Focuses on plants—including herbs, roses, irises, cacti, alpine plants—adapted to Idaho's wide range of climates. Idaho native species and hummingbird- and butterfly-attracting plants.

NEW MEXICO

Santa Fe Greenhouses/High Country Gardens
2902 Rufina Street
Santa Fe, NM 87507
(505) 473-2700
www.santafegreenhouses.com

A small but very well-designed demonstration garden at a commercial nursery actively involved in developing plants appropriate to the Rocky Mountain region and the Southwest. Guided tours in summer (check Web site for a schedule of events).

UTAH

Red Butte Garden and Arboretum
(State Arboretum of Utah)

University of Utah
300 Wakara Way
Salt Lake City, UT 84108
www.redbuttegarden.org/index.html

*One hundred and fifty acres of gardens, interpretive dis-
plays, and research facilities make this the resource for
botanical and ecological information on plants in the
Intermountain West. Also offers workshops, outings, and
events for kids.*

WYOMING

Cheyenne Botanic Gardens

710 S. Lions Park Drive
Cheyenne, WY 82001
(307) 637-6458
www.botanic.org

*A small but well-planned garden demonstrating plants
adapted to the difficult high-plains climate, as well as
greenhouses with garden crops and tropical plants. Also
offers garden therapy and community gardening pro-
grams employing seniors, youth, and disabled people as
volunteers.*

Index

Thirst-Aid and First-Aid Kit
for the Gardener's Bookshelf

XERISCAPE HAND-BOOK

A How-To Guide to Natural Resource-Wise Gardening

by Gayle Weinstein

ISBN 1-55591-346-6
$24.95 PB

XERISCAPE PLANT GUIDE

100 Water-Wise Plants for Gardens and Landscapes

by Denver Water Board

ISBN 1-55591-253-2
$27.95 PB

XERISCAPE COLOR GUIDE

100 Water-Wise Plants for Gardens and Landscapes

by David Winger

ISBN 1-55591-391-1
$15.95 PB

THE ZEN OF GARDENING IN THE HIGH AND ARID WEST

Tips, Tools, and Techniques

by David Wann

ISBN 1-55591-457-8
$17.95 PB

PESTS OF THE WEST

Prevention and Control for Today's Garden and Small Farm

by Whitney Cranshaw

ISBN 1-55591-401-2
$19.95 PB

NATIVE PLANTS FOR HIGH-ELEVATION WESTERN GARDENS

by Janice Busco and Nancy R. Morin

ISBN 1-55591-475-6
$29.95 PB

FULCRUM PUBLISHING

16100 Table Mountain Parkway, Suite 300, Golden, CO, 80403
To order call 800-992-2908 or visit www.fulcrum-gardening.com
Also available at your local bookstore or gardening center